Maths

The 13+
Study Book

For the Common Entrance 13+ exams

Practise • Prepare • Pass

Everything your child needs for 13+ success

CONTENTS

Section 1 — Numbers

Section 2 — Algebra

Section 3 — Graphs

Section 4 — Ratio, Proportion and Rates of Change

Section 5 — Geometry and Measures

Section 6 — Probability and Statistics

Published by CGP

Written by Richard Parsons.

Updated by Liam Dyer and Rob Harrison.

Editors:
Ali Palin, Sophie Scott, Ben Train, Charlotte Whiteley

With thanks to Caley Simpson for the proofreading.

ISBN: 978 1 78294 177 4

Printed by Elanders Ltd, Newcastle upon Tyne.
Clipart from Corel®

1

13+ Maths

Like it or not, you're going to be <u>tested</u> on <u>13+ Maths</u> at some point.
At least this page should shed some light on <u>what to expect</u> come exam day...

There are **Three Levels** in the **13+ Maths** Exams

1) You can either do <u>Level 1</u>, <u>Level 2</u> or <u>Level 3</u> exams for <u>Common Entrance 13+ Maths</u>.
2) Level 3 is the <u>hardest</u> level — for Levels 2 and 3 you'll need to learn <u>a bit more</u> than what's in Level 1 (see page 2).
3) You'll sit a <u>calculator</u> paper, a <u>non-calculator</u> paper and a <u>mental arithmetic</u> test.
4) If you're <u>not sure</u> what level you'll be sitting, <u>ask</u> your teacher.

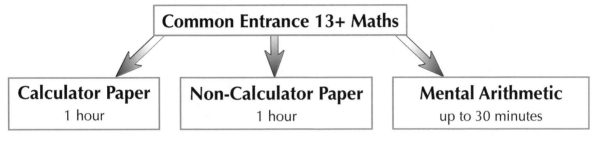

| **Calculator Paper** | **Non-Calculator Paper** | **Mental Arithmetic** |
| 1 hour | 1 hour | up to 30 minutes |

You Might Sit the **CASE Paper**

1) You may be entered for the <u>CASE paper</u> — CASE stands for <u>C</u>ommon <u>A</u>cademic <u>S</u>cholarship <u>E</u>xamination. You'll be <u>told</u> if you're sitting this paper.
2) CASE papers last for <u>1 hour 30 minutes</u>.
3) The questions in CASE papers are based on the <u>Level 3</u> subject content.
4) There are <u>two</u> sections in the exam — <u>Section A</u> and <u>Section B</u>.
   • You should answer <u>every</u> question in Section A.
   • Section B is a bit <u>harder</u>, so you might not be able to answer all the questions. It's <u>better</u> to give complete solutions to <u>some</u> questions instead of lots of <u>partial</u> solutions.

If your school sets its own 13+ exams the papers might be a bit different to what's described on this page. Ask your teacher what your papers will look like.

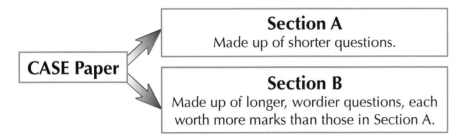

CASE Paper

Section A
Made up of shorter questions.

Section B
Made up of longer, wordier questions, each worth more marks than those in Section A.

It's **Important** to Always **Show Your Working**

1) In all of the papers apart from the mental arithmetic test, you can <u>pick up marks</u> for showing the correct <u>working</u>.
2) That means even if you make a <u>mistake</u> with the final answer, you <u>won't lose</u> all of the marks for that question.
3) It also means that if you <u>don't</u> show your working you could <u>miss out</u> on marks, even if your final answer is <u>correct</u>.
4) Make sure your working is always <u>clear</u> and <u>easy to read</u>, and you write down <u>every step</u> that you take.

Even if you use a calculator, write down each stage of the calculation.

13+ Maths

How to Use This Book

Have a look at the following information — it'll explain what everything in this book means.

What You Need to **Learn** Depends on Your **13+ Level**

- If you're doing Level 1, you only need to learn material that is marked with a Level 1 stamp — (L1)
- If you're doing Level 2, you need to learn all the Level 1 material,
  plus anything marked with a Level 2 stamp — (L2).
- If you're doing Level 3, you need to learn everything in this book.
  The Level 3 stamp marks up the extra material that's just for those doing Level 3 — (L3).

There Are Lots of **Features** to **Help** You **Learn**

This book is split up into 6 sections. Each section is split into different topics, so you can study the bits you need.

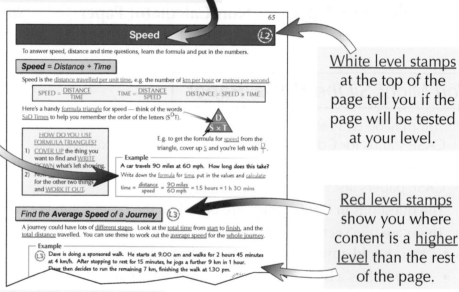

Examples work through questions on the topic you're studying. They have helpful comments explaining the working.

White level stamps at the top of the page tell you if the page will be tested at your level.

Red level stamps show you where content is a higher level than the rest of the page.

At the bottom of every page, you'll find a box with some practice questions testing the content.

Grey level stamps before a question tell you which questions are a higher level than the rest of the page.

Summary questions at the end of each section test you on what you've learnt.

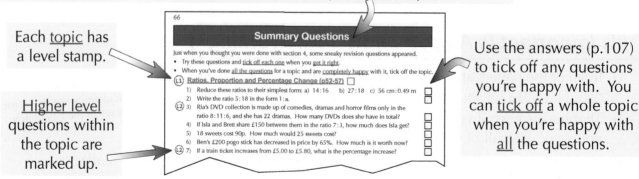

Each topic has a level stamp.

Higher level questions within the topic are marked up.

Use the answers (p.107) to tick off any questions you're happy with. You can tick off a whole topic when you're happy with all the questions.

There's also a glossary (p.103), index (p.112) and a helpful reference sheet (inside the back cover).

Calculating Tips

Here are some nifty tips and tricks that you'll need before you get going.

BODMAS

| **B**rackets, **O**ther, **D**ivision, **M**ultiplication, **A**ddition, **S**ubtraction |

BODMAS tells you the ORDER in which operations should be done: work out Brackets first, then Other things like powers, then Divide / Multiply groups of numbers before Adding or Subtracting them.

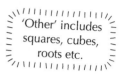
'Other' includes squares, cubes, roots etc.

Examples

Work out 4 + 6 ÷ 2

1) Follow BODMAS — do the division first...

$4 + 6 ÷ 2$
$= 4 + 3$

2) ...then the addition:

$= 7$

Calculate $10 - 2^3$

1) Start by working out the cube:

$10 - 2^3$
$= 10 - 8$

2) Then do the subtraction:

$= 2$

Example

(L2) **Find $2^3 - 6 × 4 + 9$**

1) Start by working out the cube:

$2^3 - 6 × 4 + 9$

2) And now the multiplication:

$= 8 - 6 × 4 + 9$

3) Then do the subtraction and addition in order from left to right:

$= 8 - 24 + 9$

$= -16 + 9 = -7$

If you don't follow the order of BODMAS, you get:
$4 + 6 ÷ 2 = 10 ÷ 2 = 5$

Don't Be Scared of **Wordy Questions**

You'll come across all sorts of wordy, real-life questions in your exams and you'll have to work out what the question's asking you to do. Remember:

1) READ the question carefully. Work out what bit of maths you need to answer it.

2) Underline the INFORMATION YOU NEED to answer the question — you might not have to use all the numbers they give you.

3) Write out the question IN MATHS and answer it, showing all your working clearly.

4) You can CHECK your answers by seeing if they look sensible.

Example

Caley's Clothing is having a 20% off sale on all clothing items. A shirt originally cost £25 What is the price of the shirt in the sale?

The "20% off" tells you this is a percentage change question (covered on page 56).

You need £25 (the original price) and 20% off (the percentage).
It doesn't matter what the shop is called or what the item is.

You want to take 20% off £25, so: 20% of £25 = £5   £25 − £5 = £20

Check: £20 is a bit less than £25, so that seems about right.

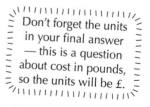
Don't forget the units in your final answer — this is a question about cost in pounds, so the units will be £.

Practice Questions

It's really important to check your working on BODMAS questions.

1) Find the value of: a) $11 - 5 × 2$ b) $12 + 8 ÷ 4$ c) $6 + 4 × 2$

(L2) 2) Find the value of: a) $3 × 6 + 15 ÷ 5$ b) $(6 × 3) ÷ 3^2$ c) $2^3 ÷ 4 + 1 × 2$

Calculating Tips

Hidden Brackets in Fractions

This is a bit of a funny one — when you have a <u>fraction</u> with <u>calculations on the top</u> or <u>bottom</u> you have to imagine they're <u>in brackets</u> and do them first.

Example

Work out $\dfrac{20 \times 5}{4 + 2 \times 3}$

1) Imagine the top and bottom are <u>both in brackets</u>. $\dfrac{(20 \times 5)}{(4 + 2 \times 3)}$

2) Now follow <u>BODMAS</u> to do the calculation. $= \dfrac{100}{(4 + 6)} = \dfrac{100}{10} = 10$

Calculators

Your calculator might be different to this one — so work out how to do everything on yours.

Make sure you know the important features on your calculator and how to use them.

Shift (or 2nd Func)

Press this <u>first</u> if you want to use something written <u>above</u> a button (e.g. the pi (π) above the $\boxed{\times 10^x}$ button).

Powers and Roots

E.g. $\boxed{4}\ \boxed{x^2}$ gives <u>4 squared = 16</u>

$\boxed{2}\ \boxed{x^\blacksquare}\ \boxed{5}$ gives <u>2 to the power 5 = 32</u>

And $\boxed{\sqrt{}}\ \boxed{25}$ gives the <u>square root</u> of <u>25 = 5</u>

Fractions

E.g. for $\frac{1}{4}$ press $\boxed{1}\ \boxed{\frac{\square}{\square}}\ \boxed{4}$.
(If you have a button that looks like $\boxed{a\frac{b}{c}}$ instead, use it in the same way.) For $1\frac{3}{5}$ press

$\boxed{1}\ \boxed{\frac{\square}{\square}}\ \boxed{3}\ \boxed{\frac{\square}{\square}}\ \boxed{5}$ (you might have to press shift first).

To <u>cancel down a fraction</u>, enter it and press $\boxed{=}$.

Pressing the $\boxed{\frac{\square}{\square}}$ or $\boxed{S \Leftrightarrow D}$ button also <u>switches</u> an answer between a <u>fraction</u> and a <u>decimal</u>.

3.6

The Answer

Before you jot down 3.6, think about <u>what it means</u>. E.g. in a money question, it might mean £3.60

Brackets

Calculators use <u>BODMAS</u> (see page 3), so if there's part of a question you want the calculator to do <u>FIRST</u> then <u>put brackets in</u> to tell it so.

(See page 72 for more on π.)

Memory (STO, RCL & M+)

E.g. for $\frac{840}{12 \times 8}$: Press $\boxed{12}\ \boxed{\times}\ \boxed{8}\ \boxed{=}$ and then $\boxed{STO}\boxed{M+}$ to store the bottom line in the memory.
Then press $\boxed{840}\ \boxed{\div}\ \boxed{RCL}\boxed{M+}\ \boxed{=}$, and the answer is **8.75**

The 'Ans' button gives the number you got when you last pressed the '=' button.

Pi (π)

The calculator stores the number for <u>pi</u> (= 3.141...). If it's <u>above</u> another button as shown here, press the $\boxed{shift}$ button <u>first</u>.

Practice Question

1) Work out $\dfrac{20 \times 8}{4 + 4 \times 3}$ using hidden brackets and BODMAS. Then try it on your calculator.

Calculating Tips

Each time you see the word 'inverse', think 'opposite' — then make sure you know how they work.

Using **Inverse Operations**

Adding and Subtracting

Adding and subtracting are <u>inverse</u> operations. Start off with a number, <u>add any number</u> to it and then <u>subtract the same number</u> — you'll be back to the number you started with.
You can use <u>inverse operations</u> to <u>check</u> your answers.

— **Example**

Simon has 26p and steals 14p from his sister Emma.
How much money does Simon have now?

<u>Add</u> the two amounts together to get the <u>total</u>.　　26 + 14 = 40p

<u>Check your answer</u> by using the <u>inverse operation</u>
— you should get the amount you started with.　　40 − 14 = 26p ✓

Multiplying and Dividing

Multiplying and dividing are inverse operations too. Start off with a number, <u>multiply it by any</u> <u>number</u> and then <u>divide by the same number</u> — you'll be back to the number you started with.

— **Example**

Michelle has 3 bags each containing 4 coconuts. She empties all of the coconuts into a box. How many coconuts are in the box?

<u>Multiply</u> the two numbers together to get the <u>total</u>.　　3 × 4 = 12 coconuts

<u>Check your answer</u> by using the <u>inverse operation</u> —
you should get the number of bags you started with.　　12 ÷ 4 = 3 bags ✓

Division by Factors

Dividing by bigger numbers without a calculator can be a bit tricky. But if you <u>break down</u> the <u>divisor</u> (the number you're dividing <u>by</u>) into <u>factors</u>, it'll make life much easier.

> Take a look on page 16 for more on factors.

— **Examples**

Work out 260 ÷ 20
1) Write 20 as the <u>product</u> of two smaller numbers (factors).　　20 = 10 × 2
2) <u>Divide</u> 260 by 10...　　260 ÷ 10 ÷ 2
3) ...and then by 2　　= 26 ÷ 2
　　= 13

Calculate 105 ÷ 15
1) Rewrite 15 as <u>two</u> smaller factors.　　15 = 5 × 3
2) Now <u>divide</u> by 5...　　105 ÷ 5 ÷ 3
3) ...and then by 3　　= 21 ÷ 3
　　= 7

> It doesn't matter what order you divide in — but it'd be a good idea to start with the easiest one.

Practice Questions

1) Use inverse operations to check your answers to the questions below.
   a) 34 + 16　　b) 108 − 59　　c) 23 × 7　　d) 156 ÷ 6
2) Use division by factors to work out the following:　a) 350 ÷ 70　　b) 80 ÷ 16

Place Value

You can use columns to work out the value of each digit in a big number or decimal.

Split **Big Numbers** into **Columns** and **Parts**

1) First, you need to know the <u>names</u> of all the <u>columns</u>. E.g. for the number <u>3 232 594</u>:

MILLIONS	HUNDRED-THOUSANDS	TEN-THOUSANDS	THOUSANDS	HUNDREDS	TENS	ONES
3	2	3	2	5	9	4

2) You can then <u>split any number up</u> into its <u>parts</u>, like this:

	3 000 000	Three million
	200 000	Two hundred thousand
	30 000	Thirty thousand
<u>Line up</u> the	2 000	Two thousand
columns so you	500	Five hundred
can read the	90	Nine tens (ninety)
numbers clearly.	4	Four ones

→ These add together to make <u>3 232 594</u>

You can also use the columns to work out the <u>value</u> of a certain digit.

> E.g. In 3 232 <u>5</u>94, the value of the <u>5</u> is <u>5 hundreds</u>.

Look at **Big Numbers** in Groups of **Three**

To <u>read</u> or <u>write</u> a <u>BIG number</u>, follow these <u>steps</u>:

1) Start from the <u>right-hand side</u> of the number →.

2) Moving <u>left</u>, ←, put a space <u>every 3 digits</u> to break it up into <u>groups of 3</u>

3) Now going <u>right</u>, →, <u>read each group of three</u> as a separate number, as shown.

> 3,232,594,
>
> MILLIONS   THOUSANDS   The rest
>
> So read as: 3 million, 232 thousand, 594
> or write fully in words:
> Three million, two hundred and thirty-two thousand, five hundred and ninety-four.

Split **Decimals** into **Decimal Places**

1) The <u>decimal places</u> have <u>names</u> too. E.g. for the number <u>173.753</u>:

HUNDREDS	TENS	ONES	DECIMAL POINT	TENTHS	HUNDREDTHS	THOUSANDTHS
1	7	3	.	7	5	3

2) You can <u>split up decimals</u> into <u>parts</u> too:

With decimals,	100,000	One hundred
line up the	70,000	Seven tens (seventy)
decimal points.	3,000	Three ones
	0,700	Seven tenths
	0,050	Five hundredths
	0,003	Three thousandths

→ These add together to make <u>173.753</u>

You can work out the <u>value</u> of a certain digit.

> E.g. In 173.7<u>5</u>3, the value of the <u>5</u> is <u>5 hundredths</u>.

Practice Questions

1) Write these numbers out fully in words: a) 9 905 285   b) 6 054 203
2) Write down in words: a) the value of the 6 in 0.684   b) the value of the 7 in 4.357

Ordering Numbers

Here's a page filled with easy examples — it's all about ordering numbers.

Ordering **Whole Numbers**

Ascending order means smallest to largest.
Descending order means largest to smallest.

— **Example** —

Write these numbers in ascending order: −53   53   17   2321   −754   421   548   −88   1729

1) First put them into groups with the <u>negative ones first</u>:

negative	2-digit	3-digit	4-digit
−53 −754 −88	53 17	421 548	2321 1729

2) Then just put each separate group in <u>order of size</u> from smallest to largest.

    −754   −88   −53   17   53   421   548   1729   2321

Ordering **Decimals**

You can also use number lines for ordering numbers.

1) Do the <u>whole number bit first</u>, then the bit <u>after the decimal point</u>.
2) If two numbers have the <u>same whole number</u> bit, order them by the <u>next digit</u>, etc.

— **Example** —

Write these numbers in order, from smallest to largest:

    0.62   18.42   0.062   0.58   0.006   18.56   8.4

1) First order them by the whole number bit from smallest to largest.

    0.62   0.062   0.58   0.006   8.4   18.42   18.56

2) Now order each whole number group by the first number
after the decimal point from smallest to largest.

    0.062   0.006   0.58   0.62   8.4   18.42   18.56

3) 0.062 and 0.006 have the same first number after the decimal point,
so keep going and compare their second numbers. Order them by size.

    0.006   0.062   0.58   0.62   8.4   18.42   18.56

Greater Than and Less Than

These <u>symbols</u> are used to show if something
is <u>bigger</u> (or <u>smaller</u>) than <u>something else</u>.

Symbol	Meaning
>	Greater than
<	Less than
≥	Greater than or equal to
≤	Less than or equal to

— **Example** —

Which of these statements is true?   a) 5 > 7   b) 6 < 3   c) 2 ≥ 2

a) 5 > 7 means 5 is <u>greater than</u> 7, which is false.   b) 6 < 3 means 6 is <u>less than</u> 3, which is false.
c) 2 ≥ 2 means 2 is <u>greater than or equal to</u> 2 — they are both <u>equal</u> so this statement is true.

Practice Questions

1) Put these numbers in descending order: 35   318   −16   −24   107   −6   −5   −115
2) Write > or < to complete the expressions: a) 30 000 _____ 29 950   b) 0.005 _____ 0.045

Section 1 — Numbers

Addition and Subtraction

I'm sure you're all chomping at the bit to learn some methods of addition and subtraction.

Adding

1) Line up the <u>ones</u> columns of each number.

2) Add up the columns from <u>right to left</u>.

3) <u>Carry over</u> any spare tens to the next column.

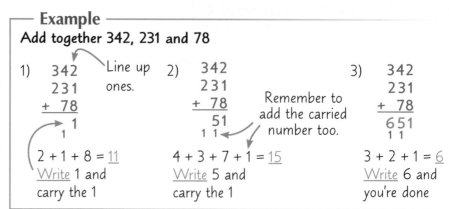

Example

Add together 342, 231 and 78

1)
```
    342    Line up
    231    ones.
  +  78
       1
     1
```
2 + 1 + 8 = 11
<u>Write</u> 1 and carry the 1

2)
```
    342
    231
  +  78
      51
    1 1
```
Remember to add the carried number too.
4 + 3 + 7 + 1 = 15
<u>Write</u> 5 and carry the 1

3)
```
    342
    231
  +  78
     651
    1 1
```
3 + 2 + 1 = 6
<u>Write</u> 6 and you're done

Subtracting

1) Line up the <u>ones</u> columns of each number.

2) Working <u>right to left</u>, subtract the <u>bottom</u> number from the <u>top</u> number.

3) If the top number is <u>smaller</u> than the bottom number, <u>borrow</u> 10 from the left.

Example

Work out 372 − 324

1)
```
      6 12
    3 7̶ 2     Line up
  − 3 2 4     ones.
```
You can't do 2 − 4, so <u>borrow 10</u> from the left.

2)
```
      6 12
    3 7̶ 2̶
  − 3 2 4
    0 4 8    12 − 4 = 8
             6 − 2 = 4
    3 − 3 = 0
```

And with **Decimals**...

The <u>method is just the same</u>, but start instead by lining up the <u>decimal points</u>.

Examples

Work out 0.7 + 32.2 + 1.65

1)
```
    0.7 0     Decimal points lined up
  3 2.2 0     It often helps to write in
  + 1.6 5     extra zeros to make all the
     .5 5     decimals the same length
    1
```
7 + 2 + 6 = 15 — write 5 and carry the 1

2)
```
    0.7 0
  3 2.2 0
  + 1.6 5
  3 4.5 5
    1
```
0 + 2 + 1 + carried 1 = 4

Ben has £5 and spends 91p on a pie. How much does he have left?

1)
```
    £ 5.0 0    Decimal points lined up
  − £ 0.9 1    0 is smaller than 1,
             so you can't do 0 − 1
```

2)
```
      4 10
    £ 5̶.0 0    Borrow 10...
  − £ 0.9 1
```

3)
```
        9
      4 1̶0 10
    £ 5̶.0̶ 0̶    ...then borrow 10 again
  − £ 0.9 1     10 − 1 = 9
    £ 4.0 9     9 − 9 = 0
               4 − 0 = 4
```

Practice Questions

1) a) 113 + 645 + 39   b) 1239 − 387   c) 0.58 + 1.47 + 16.4
2) Rob beat his 100 m sprint time of 13.22 seconds by 0.87 seconds. What is his new best time?

Multiplying by 10, 100, etc.

This stuff is easy peasy — I'm sure you'll have no problem flying through this page.

1) To **Multiply** Any Number by **10**

Move all the digits <u>ONE</u> place <u>BIGGER</u> and if it's needed, <u>ADD A ZERO</u> on the end.

E.g. $1.6 \times 10 = 1\,6$

$6213 \times 10 = 6\,2\,1\,3\,0$

$672.12 \times 10 = 6\,7\,2\,1\,.\,2$

2) To **Multiply** Any Number by **100**

Move all the digits <u>TWO</u> places <u>BIGGER</u> and <u>ADD ZEROS</u> if necessary.

Add zeros up to the decimal point.

E.g. $3.5 \times 100 = 3\,5\,0$

$78 \times 100 = 7\,8\,0\,0$

$3.7734 \times 100 = 3\,7\,7\,.\,3\,4$

3) To **Multiply** by **1000**, the Same Rule Applies:

Move all the digits <u>THREE</u> places <u>BIGGER</u> and <u>ADD ZEROS</u> if necessary.

E.g. $99.67 \times 1000 = 9\,9\,6\,7\,0$

$8.4 \times 1000 = 8\,4\,0\,0$

You always <u>move</u> all the <u>DIGITS</u> this much:

<u>1 place for 10</u>,   <u>2 places for 100</u>,
<u>3 places for 1000</u>,   etc.

The number of zeros tells you the number of places to move.

4) To **Multiply** by Numbers like **20, 300, 8000** etc.

<u>MULTIPLY</u> by <u>2</u> or <u>3</u> or <u>8</u> etc. <u>FIRST</u>,
then move all the digits so many places <u>BIGGER</u> (⟵)
according to how many zeros there are.

— **Example** —

Calculate 110 × 500

1) First multiply by 5... $110 \times 5 = 550$
2) ...then move the digits 2 places bigger. $550 \times 100 = 55000$

Practice Questions

1) Work out: a) 6.4×10 b) 852×100 c) 0.0885×1000 d) 5.4×50 e) 3.2×600
2) A type of centipede has 200 legs. How many legs do 16 of these centipedes have altogether?

Section 1 — Numbers

Dividing by 10, 100, etc.

This is pretty easy stuff too. Just make sure you know it — that's all.

1) To **Divide** Any Number by **10**

Move all the digits <u>ONE</u> place <u>SMALLER</u> and if it's needed, <u>REMOVE ZEROS</u> at the end of the decimal part.

E.g. $32.2 \div 10 = 3 . 2\ 2$

$6541 \div 10 = 6\ 5\ 4 . 1$

$4200 \div 10 = 4\ 2\ 0 . \emptyset = 4\ 2\ 0$

2) To **Divide** Any Number by **100**

Move all the digits <u>TWO</u> places <u>SMALLER</u> and <u>REMOVE ANY ZEROS</u> at the end of the decimal part.

E.g. $333.8 \div 100 = 3 . 3\ 3\ 8$

$160 \div 100 = 1 . 6\ \emptyset = 1 . 6$

$1729 \div 100 = 1\ 7 . 2\ 9$

3) To **Divide** by **1000**, the Same Rule Applies:

Move all the digits <u>THREE</u> places <u>SMALLER</u> and <u>REMOVE ANY ZEROS</u> at the end of the decimal part.

E.g. $6587 \div 1000 = 6 . 5\ 8\ 7$

$234 \div 1000 = 0 . 2\ 3\ 4$

You always <u>move</u> all the <u>DIGITS</u> this much:

<u>1 place for 10</u>,   <u>2 places for 100</u>,
<u>3 places for 1000</u>,   etc.

The number of zeros tells you the number of places to move.

4) To **Divide** by Numbers like **40, 300, 7000** etc.

<u>DIVIDE</u> by <u>4</u> or <u>3</u> or <u>7</u> etc. <u>FIRST</u>, then move all the digits so many places <u>SMALLER</u> (i.e. to the right ⟶) according to how many zeros there are.

— Example —

Calculate 180 ÷ 200

1)   First divide by 2... $180 \div 2 = 90$

2)   ...then move the digits 2 places smaller. $90 \div 100 = 0.90 = 0.9$

Practice Questions

1)   Work out: a) 8.59 ÷ 10   b) 35698 ÷ 100   c) 67.52 ÷ 1000   d) 2080 ÷ 20
2)   Milly has 6798 shiny 1p coins. How much is this in pounds and pence?

Multiplying Without a Calculator

Multiplying with a calculator is a piece of cake. The real challenge is multiplying without one.

Multiplying by a **One-Digit Number**

Just follow these steps to multiply a big number by a one-digit number:

1) Write out the calculation with the big number on top and line up the place value columns.

2) Multiply the one-digit number by each part of the big number in turn.
   Start with the place value column of least value (it's always the one on the right).

3) Each time you get an answer of 10 or more, record the first digit of the answer below the
   next column (like you do when you're adding). You'll add this onto the next multiplication.

> **Example**
>
> Work out 327 × 3
>
> 1) 3 2 7
>   ×   3   7 × 3 = 21, so put a
>   ‾‾‾‾‾   1 here and a 2 under
>   1   the next column.
>   2
>
> 2) 3 2 7
>   ×   3   2 × 3 = 6
>   ‾‾‾‾‾   Add the extra
>   8 1   2 to get 8
>   2
>
> 3) 3 2 7
>   ×   3   Finish by
>   ‾‾‾‾‾   multiplying
>   9 8 1   3 × 3
>   2

Multiplying by **Bigger Numbers**

There are lots of methods you can use for this. Two popular ones are shown below.

> **Example**
>
> Calculate 48 × 33
>
> ### The Traditional Method
>
> Split it into
> separate   4 8
> multiplications,   × 3 3   This is 3 × 48
> then add up the   1 4,4
> results in columns 1 4,4 0 ← This is 30 × 48
> (from right to left). 1 5 8 4
>   This is 144 + 1440
>
> ### The Grid Method
>
> 1) Split up each number into its ones and tens
>   (and hundreds and thousands if it has them).
>   48 = 40 + 8 and 33 = 30 + 3
>
> 2) Draw a grid, with
>   the 'bits' of the
>   numbers round the
>   outside.
>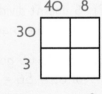
>
> 3) Multiply the bits
>   round the edge to
>   fill each square.
>
> | | 40 | 8 |
> |------|------|-----|
> | 30 | 1200 | 240 |
> | 3 | 120 | 24 |
>
>   40 × 30   40 × 3   8 × 30   8 × 3
>
> 4) Finally, add up
>   the numbers in
>   the squares.
>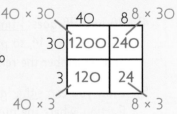
>    ```
>      1200
>       240
>       120
>    +   24
>    ‾‾‾‾‾‾‾
>      1584
>    ```

> **Example**
>
> Aston ate 16 almonds every day for 132 days.
> How many almonds did he eat in total?
>
> ```
>     1 3 2
>   ×   1 6     This is 6 × 132
>   ‾‾‾‾‾‾‾
>     7 9 2
>   1 3 2 0  ← This is 10 × 132
>   ‾‾‾‾‾‾‾
>   2 1 1 2  ← This is 792 + 1320
> ```
>
> So Aston ate 2112 almonds.

Practice Question

Two different multiplication methods — try them out on these questions to see which you prefer.
1) Work out   a) 472 × 8   b) 42 × 37   c) 509 × 64

Dividing Without a Calculator

OK, time for some dividing without a calculator — ready for another challenge?

Short Division

The **Easy** Case — **Exact Division**

You'll find it helpful to write out the first few multiples (see p.16) of the number you're dividing by.

When a division gives a <u>whole number</u> answer — it's pretty simple.

— **Example** —

What is 848 ÷ 16?

1) Set out the division as shown.

$$16 \overline{)848}$$

2) Look at the first digit under the line. 8 doesn't divide by 16, so <u>put a zero</u> above and look at the <u>next digit</u>.

$$16 \overline{)848}$$ → 0 above

3) 16 × 5 = 80, so 16 into 84 goes <u>5 times</u>, with a <u>remainder</u> of 84 − 80 = 4

carry the remainder

$$16 \overline{)84^48}$$ → 05

4) 16 into 48 goes <u>3 times exactly</u>.

the top line has the final answer

$$16 \overline{)8\,4^48}$$ → 053

So 848 ÷ 16 = 53

Multiples of 16:
16 × 1 = 16
16 × 2 = 32
16 × 3 = 48
16 × 4 = 64
16 × 5 = 80

The **Tricky** Case — **Non-Exact Division**

When the division <u>doesn't</u> give a nice number, you can give your answer in <u>several</u> different ways.

— **Example** —

What is 658 ÷ 28?

1) Set out the division as shown.

$$28 \overline{)658}$$

2) 6 doesn't divide by 28, so <u>write a zero</u> above the 6 and look at the <u>next digit</u>.

$$28 \overline{)658}$$ → 023

3) 28 into 65 goes <u>2 times</u> with a <u>remainder</u> of 65 − 56 = 9, so put a <u>2</u> above the 5

carry the remainder

$$28 \overline{)65^98}$$ → 023

4) 28 into 98 goes <u>3 times</u> with a <u>remainder</u> of 98 − 84 = 14, so put a <u>3</u> above the 8 and remember the remainder of 14

$$28 \overline{)65^98}$$ → 023

Knowing the remainder is useful if you want to know how many of something is left after a division.

5) Now you can <u>either</u> give your answer as a <u>mixed fraction</u>, where the numerator is the <u>remainder</u> and the denominator is the <u>number you're dividing by</u>...

Either $658 \div 28 = 23 \frac{14}{28}$ ← remainder

number you're dividing by

6) ...or keep going to give it as a <u>decimal</u>. Keep adding <u>zeros</u> after the decimal point and carry on. 28 goes into 140 exactly <u>5 times</u>, so you're done.

$$28 \overline{)65^98^{14}0}$$ → 023.5

Or $658 \div 28 = 23.5$

Multiples of 28:
28 × 1 = 28
28 × 2 = 56
28 × 3 = 84
28 × 4 = 112
28 × 5 = 140

Practice Questions

1) Work out   a) 128 ÷ 8   b) 418 ÷ 19   c) 550 ÷ 44

2) Cyril shares 150 gummy worms equally among 12 friends. How many are left over?

Multiplying and Dividing with Decimals

On the last two pages you've seen how to multiply and divide whole numbers without a calculator. Well, decimals are the same if you just ignore the decimal points — worry about them at the end.

Multiplying Decimals

1) Start by <u>ignoring</u> the decimal points. Do the multiplication using <u>whole numbers</u>.
2) Count the <u>total</u> number of digits after the <u>decimal points</u> in the original numbers.
3) Make the answer have the <u>same number</u> of decimal places.

— **Example** —

Work out 4.8 × 1.64

1) Do the <u>whole-number</u> multiplication: $\qquad$ 48 × 164 = 7872

$\quad$ *Take a look at page 11 for multiplying whole numbers.*

2) Count the digits <u>after</u> the decimal points: $\quad$ 4.<u>8</u> × 1.<u>64</u> has <u>3 digits</u> after the decimal points — so will the answer.

3) Give the answer the <u>same number</u> of decimal places: $\quad$ 4.8 × 1.64 = 7.872

Dividing a Decimal by a Whole Number

For these, you just set the question out like a whole number division <u>but</u> put the <u>decimal point</u> in the answer <u>right above</u> the one in the question.

— **Example** —

What is 49.8 ÷ 6?

1) Put the <u>decimal point</u> in the answer above the one in the question.

$$6\ |\ 4\ 9\ .\ 8 \qquad 6\ \underline{4\ 9}\ .^1 8 \qquad 6\ |\ 4\ 9\ .\ ^1 8$$

2) 6 into 4 <u>doesn't go</u>, so <u>put a zero</u> above and look at the <u>next digit</u>.

3) 6 goes into 49 <u>8 times</u>, so carry the <u>remainder of 1</u>

4) 6 goes into 18 <u>3 times exactly</u>. So 49.8 ÷ 6 = 8.3

Dividing a Number by a Decimal

Two-for-one here — this works if you're dividing a whole number (or a decimal) by a decimal.

— **Example** —

What is 8.48 ÷ 0.16?

1) The trick here is to write it <u>as a fraction</u>: $\quad 8.48 \div 0.16 = \dfrac{8.48}{0.16}$

2) <u>Get rid of the decimals</u> by multiplying top and bottom by 100 (see p.9): $\quad = \dfrac{848}{16}$

$\quad$ *Any number will get bigger when you divide by a number between 0 and 1 and get smaller when you multiply by a number between 0 and 1*

3) It's now a <u>decimal-free</u> division that you know how to solve: $\quad = 53$

$\quad$ *This is worked out on the previous page.*

Practice Questions

1) Work out: $\quad$ a) 2.87 × 42 $\quad$ b) 17.32 × 0.15 $\quad$ c) 5.1 ÷ 5

(L2) 2) If one apple costs £0.32, how many apples can James buy with £20.48?

(L2) 3) Work out 83.2 ÷ 0.13

Negative Numbers

Numbers less than zero are negative. You can add, subtract, multiply and divide with them.

Adding and Subtracting with Negative Numbers

Use the <u>number line</u> for <u>addition</u> and <u>subtraction</u> involving negative numbers:

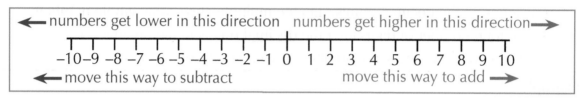

←numbers get lower in this direction   numbers get higher in this direction→

−10 −9 −8 −7 −6 −5 −4 −3 −2 −1 0 1 2 3 4 5 6 7 8 9 10

←move this way to subtract   move this way to add →

Examples

Number lines can sometimes have different scales. E.g. they might go up in steps of 5

What is −3 + 5?   Start at −3 and move 5 places in the positive direction:

−4 −3 −2 −1 0 1 2 3   So −3 + 5 = 2

Work out 3 − 6   Start at 3 and move 6 places in the negative direction:

−4 −3 −2 −1 0 1 2 3 4   So 3 − 6 = −3

What temperature is 5 °C colder than −1 °C?   Start at −1 and move 5 places in the negative direction:

−6 −5 −4 −3 −2 −1 0 °C   −6 °C

Use These Rules for Combining Signs

These rules are <u>ONLY TO BE USED WHEN</u>:

+	+	makes	+
+	−	makes	−
−	+	makes	−
−	−	makes	+

1) <u>Multiplying</u> or <u>dividing</u>

Example

Find: —(invisible + sign)
a) −3 × 5   − + makes −   so −3 × 5 = −15
b) −18 ÷ −3   − − makes +   so −18 ÷ −3 = 6

2) <u>Two signs</u> appear <u>next to</u> each other

Example

Work out:
a) 2 + −8   + − makes −   so 2 + −8 = 2 − 8 = −6
b) 3 − −9   − − makes +   so 3 − −9 = 3 + 9 = 12

Practice Questions

Combining signs — if they're the same it makes + and if they're different it makes −.

1) Work out: a) −6 + 11   b) −5 − 10   c) −3 × −6   d) 21 ÷ −7

2) L3 On Friday, the temperature in Negaton was −5.6 °C and in Tiverville was −19.7 °C. What was the difference in temperature between Negaton and Tiverville?

Prime Numbers

L1

There's a special type of number you need to know about — the prime numbers...

Prime Numbers Don't Divide by Anything

Prime numbers are all the numbers that only come up in their own times table:

2 3 5 7 11 13 17 19 23 29 31 37...

The only way to get ANY PRIME NUMBER is: 1 × ITSELF

E.g. The only numbers that multiply to give 3 are 1 × 3
The only numbers that multiply to give 19 are 1 × 19

Example

Show that 18 is not a prime number.

Just find another way to make 18 other than 1 × 18: 3 × 6 = 18

18 divides by other numbers apart from 1 and 18, so it isn't a prime number.

Five Important Facts

1) 1 is NOT a prime number.
2) 2 is the ONLY even prime number.
3) The first four prime numbers are 2, 3, 5 and 7
4) Prime numbers end in 1, 3, 7 or 9 (2 and 5 are the only exceptions to this rule).
5) But NOT ALL numbers ending in 1, 3, 7 or 9 are primes, as shown here:
(Only the circled ones are primes.)

②	③	⑤	⑦
⑪	⑬	⑰	⑲
21	㉓	27	㉙
㉛	33	㊲	39
㊶	㊸	㊼	49
51	(53)	57	(59)
(61)	63	(67)	69

How to Find Prime Numbers — a very simple method

1) All primes (above 5) end in 1, 3, 7 or 9 — ignore any numbers that don't end in one of those.
2) To find which of them ACTUALLY ARE primes you only need to divide each one by 3 and 7
If it doesn't divide exactly by either 3 or 7 then it's a prime.

This only works for primes up to 120

Example

Find all the prime numbers in this list: 51, 52, 53, 54, 55, 56, 57, 58, 59

1) Get rid of anything that doesn't end in 1, 3, 7 or 9: 51, ~~52~~, 53, ~~54~~, ~~55~~, ~~56~~, 57, ~~58~~, 59

2) Now try dividing 51, 53, 57 and 59 by 3 and 7:
51 ÷ 3 = 17 so 51 is NOT a prime number
53 ÷ 3 = 17.666... and 53 ÷ 7 = 7.571... so 53 is a prime number
57 ÷ 3 = 19 so 57 is NOT a prime number
59 ÷ 3 = 19.666... and 59 ÷ 7 = 8.428... so 59 is a prime number
So the prime numbers in the list are 53 and 59

Practice Question

1) Write down all the prime numbers from this list: 49, 63, 38, 73, 77, 16, 39, 83

Multiples, Factors and Prime Factors

Ah, welcome to the lovely world of factors — pull up a seat and get ready to learn.

Multiples and Factors

The MULTIPLES of a number are just the values in its times table.

— **Example** —
Find the first 5 multiples of 12
You just need to find the first 5 numbers in the 12 times table: 12   24   36   48   60

The FACTORS of a number are all the numbers that divide into it exactly.   Here's how to find them:

— **Example** —
Find all the factors of 28

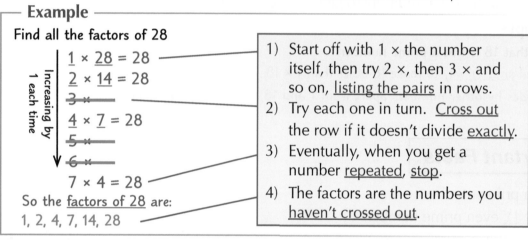

$1 \times 28 = 28$
$2 \times 14 = 28$
~~3 ×~~
$4 \times 7 = 28$
~~5 ×~~
~~6 ×~~
$7 \times 4 = 28$

Increasing by 1 each time

So the factors of 28 are:
1, 2, 4, 7, 14, 28

1) Start off with 1 × the number itself, then try 2 ×, then 3 × and so on, listing the pairs in rows.
2) Try each one in turn.   Cross out the row if it doesn't divide exactly.
3) Eventually, when you get a number repeated, stop.
4) The factors are the numbers you haven't crossed out.

Finding Prime Factors — The Factor Tree

Any whole number can be written as a string of prime numbers all multiplied together — this is called a product of prime factors.   The easiest way to find it is using a factor tree.

— **Example** —
Write 280 as a product of its prime factors.

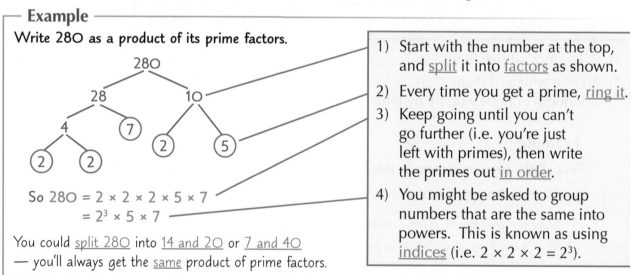

So 280 = 2 × 2 × 2 × 5 × 7
    $= 2^3 \times 5 \times 7$

You could split 280 into 14 and 20 or 7 and 40 — you'll always get the same product of prime factors.

1) Start with the number at the top, and split it into factors as shown.
2) Every time you get a prime, ring it.
3) Keep going until you can't go further (i.e. you're just left with primes), then write the primes out in order.
4) You might be asked to group numbers that are the same into powers.   This is known as using indices (i.e. $2 \times 2 \times 2 = 2^3$).

The prime factors of a number are always the same, no matter how you split it up.

Practice Questions

1) Find: a) The first 8 multiples of 15   b) All the factors of 64
2) Write down the next two numbers in the number pattern 12, 24, 36, 48, ...
3) a) Write 300 as a product of its prime factors.   b) Write your answer to a) using indices.

Section 1 — Numbers

LCM and HCF

Here are two big fancy names for you — but don't be put off, they're both easy.

LCM — 'Lowest Common Multiple'

'Lowest Common Multiple' sounds a bit complicated, but all it means is this:

> The SMALLEST number that will DIVIDE BY ALL the numbers in question.

Method

LIST the MULTIPLES of ALL the numbers. Find the SMALLEST one that's in ALL the lists.

OR

Write out the PRODUCT OF PRIME FACTORS of each number. PAIR UP numbers that appear in BOTH PRODUCTS, and CROSS OUT one of each pair. Then MULTIPLY all the others together.

Examples

Find the smallest number that will divide by 3 and 4.

Multiples of 3: 3, 6, 9, (12,) 15, ...

Multiples of 4: 4, 8, (12,) 16, ...

So the smallest number that will divide 3 and 4 is 12

Find the lowest common multiple (LCM) of 20 and 28.

20 = 2 × 2 × 5

28 = 2 × 2 × 7

So the LCM of 20 and 28 is 2 × 2 × 5 × 7 = 140

This method's handy when the two numbers are quite big.

HCF — 'Highest Common Factor'

'Highest Common Factor' — all it means is this:

> The BIGGEST number that will DIVIDE INTO ALL the numbers in question.

Method

LIST the FACTORS of ALL the numbers. Find the BIGGEST one that's in ALL the lists.

OR

Write out the PRODUCT OF PRIME FACTORS of each number. CIRCLE the numbers that appear in BOTH PRODUCTS, then MULTIPLY these numbers together.

Examples

Find the biggest number that will divide into 24, 42 and 84.

Factors of 24 are: 1, 2, 3, 4, (6,) 8, 12, 24

Factors of 42 are: 1, 2, 3, (6,) 7, 14, 21, 42

Factors of 84 are: 1, 2, 3, 4, (6,) 7, 12, 14, 21, 28, 42, 84

So the biggest number that will divide into 24, 42 and 84 is 6

Find the highest common factor (HCF) of 60 and 220.

60 = 2 × 2 × 3 × 5

220 = 2 × 2 × 5 × 11

So the highest common factor (HCF) of 60 and 220 is 2 × 2 × 5 = 20

Only use the numbers from each pair once.

Practice Questions

1) Find the smallest number that will divide by 9 and 12

2) Find the highest common factor of 48, 64 and 80

Fractions, Decimals and Percentages

Fractions, decimals and percentages are three different ways of describing when you've got part of a whole thing. They're closely related and you can convert between them.

This table shows some really common conversions — it'll help you if you know them straight off:

Fraction	Decimal	Percentage
$\frac{1}{2}$	0.5	50%
$\frac{1}{4}$	0.25	25%
$\frac{3}{4}$	0.75	75%
$\frac{1}{8}$	0.125	$12\frac{1}{2}\%$
$\frac{1}{3}$	0.333333...	$33\frac{1}{3}\%$
$\frac{2}{3}$	0.666666...	$66\frac{2}{3}\%$
$\frac{1}{10}$	0.1	10%
$\frac{1}{5}$	0.2	20%
$\frac{2}{5}$	0.4	40%

Fractions with a 1 on the top (e.g. $\frac{1}{2}, \frac{1}{3}, \frac{1}{4}$, etc.) are called unit fractions.

0.3333... and 0.6666... are known as 'recurring' decimals — the same pattern of numbers carries on repeating itself forever. You might see them written as $0.\dot{3}$ and $0.\dot{6}$.

The more of those conversions you learn, the better — but for those that you <u>don't know</u>, you must <u>also learn</u> how to <u>convert</u> between the three types. These are the methods:

Fraction —— Divide ——→ Decimal —— × by 100 ——→ Percentage

E.g. $\frac{7}{20}$ is 7÷20   = 0.35   E.g. 0.35 × 100   = 35%

Fraction ←—— The awkward one —— Decimal ←—— ÷ by 100 —— Percentage

<u>Converting decimals to fractions</u> is a bit more awkward.
The digits after the decimal point go on the top, and a <u>power of 10</u> on the bottom — with the same number of zeros as there were decimal places.

$0.6 = \frac{6}{10}$ $0.3 = \frac{3}{10}$ $0.7 = \frac{7}{10}$ etc.

$0.12 = \frac{12}{100}$ $0.78 = \frac{78}{100}$ $0.05 = \frac{5}{100}$ etc.

$0.345 = \frac{345}{1000}$ $0.908 = \frac{908}{1000}$ $0.024 = \frac{24}{1000}$ etc.

These can often be <u>cancelled down</u> — see p.19

Practice Questions

Learn the stuff in the top table and the 4 conversion processes. Then it's time for some questions.

1) Turn the following decimals into fractions and reduce them to their simplest form.
   a) 0.8   b) 0.04   c) 0.23   d) 0.999

2) Which is greater: a) 22% or $\frac{3}{9}$ b) 0.7 or $\frac{17}{25}$?

3) Write these in ascending order: 0.5, 55%, $\frac{1}{5}$

Fractions

This page tells you how to deal with fractions without your calculator.

Equivalent Fractions

$\frac{1}{4}$ ...is equivalent to... $\frac{4}{16}$

1) Equivalent fractions are equal in size...

2) ...but the numbers on the top and bottom are different.

3) To get from one fraction to an equivalent one —
   MULTIPLY top and bottom by the SAME NUMBER.

$$\overset{\times 2}{\frac{1}{2}} = \frac{2}{4} \qquad \overset{\times 5}{\frac{3}{4}} = \frac{15}{20} \qquad \overset{\times 100}{\frac{1}{5}} = \frac{100}{500}$$
$$\underset{\times 2}{} \qquad \underset{\times 5}{} \qquad \underset{\times 100}{}$$

Cancelling Down

1) You sometimes need to simplify a fraction by 'cancelling down'.

2) This means DIVIDING top and bottom by the SAME NUMBER.

3) To get the fraction as simple as possible,
   you might have to do this more than once.

4) When you can't divide any more the fraction
   is said to be in its simplest form, or lowest terms.

$$\overset{\div 10}{\underset{\div 10}{\frac{20}{40}}} = \overset{\div 2}{\underset{\div 2}{\frac{2}{4}}} = \frac{1}{2}$$

$$\overset{\div 3}{\underset{\div 3}{\frac{3}{15}}} = \frac{1}{5}$$

Ordering Fractions

E.g. Which is bigger, $\frac{2}{3}$ or $\frac{3}{4}$?

$$\overset{\times 4}{\underset{\times 4}{\frac{2}{3}}} = \frac{8}{12} \qquad \overset{\times 3}{\underset{\times 3}{\frac{3}{4}}} = \frac{9}{12}$$

1) Look at the bottom numbers ('denominators') of
   the fractions: 3 and 4

2) Think of a number they will both go into — try 12

3) Change each fraction (make equivalent fractions)
   so the bottom number is 12

4) Now check which is bigger by looking at their
   top numbers ('numerators').

5) 9 is bigger than 8, so $\frac{3}{4}$ is bigger than $\frac{2}{3}$

Mixed Numbers

Mixed numbers have an integer part and a fraction part. Just turn
them into improper fractions first, then you can use them as normal.

In an improper fraction, the top number is larger than the bottom number.

Examples

Write $3\frac{4}{5}$ as an improper fraction.

1) Think of the mixed number as an addition:
$$3\frac{4}{5} = 3 + \frac{4}{5}$$

2) Turn the integer part into a fraction:
$$3 + \frac{4}{5} = \frac{15}{5} + \frac{4}{5} = \frac{15+4}{5} = \frac{19}{5}$$

Write $\frac{23}{3}$ as a mixed number.

Divide the top number by the bottom.

1) The answer gives the whole number part.

2) The remainder goes on top of the fraction.

$$23 \div 3 = 7 \text{ remainder } 2 \quad \text{so} \quad \frac{23}{3} = 7\frac{2}{3}$$

Practice Questions

Have a go at cancelling down and ordering the fractions below — and no cheating with a calculator.

1) Cancel these down as far as possible: a) $\frac{20}{28}$ b) $\frac{9}{36}$

2) Which is bigger, $\frac{5}{8}$ or $\frac{2}{3}$?   3) Write $\frac{43}{7}$ as a mixed number.

Fractions

Adding and Subtracting

1) If the <u>bottom numbers</u> are the <u>same</u>, add or subtract the <u>TOP NUMBERS ONLY</u>, leaving the bottom number <u>as it is</u>.

2) If the bottom numbers are <u>different</u>, you have to <u>make them the same</u> using <u>equivalent fractions</u> (see page 19).

Examples

Calculate $\frac{5}{7} - \frac{3}{7}$

Just <u>subtract</u> the top numbers. Keep the bottom number the <u>same</u>.

$$\frac{5}{7} - \frac{3}{7} = \frac{5-3}{7} = \frac{2}{7}$$

Calculate $\frac{1}{4} + \frac{5}{12}$

1) Convert the fractions so they have the <u>same denominator</u>.
$$\frac{1}{4} = \frac{3}{12}$$

2) Then <u>add</u> as usual.
$$\frac{3}{12} + \frac{5}{12} = \frac{3+5}{12} = \frac{8}{12} = \frac{2}{3}$$

It's a good idea to try and give your answer in its simplest form.

Multiplying

1) <u>Multiply</u> the <u>top numbers</u> to find the <u>numerator</u>...

2) ...and <u>multiply</u> the <u>bottom numbers</u> to find the <u>denominator</u>.

Example

Calculate $7 \times \frac{2}{5}$

1) Write the whole number as a <u>fraction</u> over 1
$$7 \times \frac{2}{5} = \frac{7}{1} \times \frac{2}{5}$$

2) Multiply the <u>top</u> and <u>bottom</u> numbers. $= \frac{14}{5}$

Examples

(L2) Calculate $\frac{3}{5} \times \frac{4}{6}$

Multiply the <u>top</u> and <u>bottom</u> numbers.

$$\frac{3}{5} \times \frac{4}{6} = \frac{3\times4}{5\times6} = \frac{12}{30} = \frac{2}{5}$$

(L2) Calculate $2\frac{1}{5} \times 4\frac{1}{2}$

1) Write both fractions as <u>improper fractions</u>.
$$2\frac{1}{5} = \frac{11}{5} \text{ and } 4\frac{1}{2} = \frac{9}{2}$$

2) Then <u>multiply</u> as usual.
$$\frac{11}{5} \times \frac{9}{2} = \frac{11\times9}{5\times2} = \frac{99}{10} \text{ or } 9\frac{9}{10}$$

Dividing

1) Turn the 2nd fraction <u>UPSIDE DOWN</u>...

2) ...and then <u>multiply</u>, as shown above.

Numbers turned upside down are called reciprocals. The reciprocal of $\frac{6}{7}$ is $\frac{7}{6}$ and the reciprocal of 3 is $\frac{1}{3}$.

Examples

Calculate $4 \div \frac{8}{3}$

1) Find the <u>reciprocal</u> of $\frac{8}{3}$
$$\frac{8}{3} \rightarrow \frac{3}{8}$$

It always helps to cancel down your fractions before multiplying.

2) Then <u>multiply</u> as usual.
$$4 \times \frac{3}{8} = \frac{\overset{1}{\cancel{4}}}{1} \times \frac{3}{\underset{2}{\cancel{8}}} = \frac{1}{1} \times \frac{3}{2} = \frac{1\times3}{1\times2} = \frac{3}{2}$$

(L3) Calculate $2\frac{4}{5} \div 3\frac{2}{3}$

1) Write both fractions as <u>improper fractions</u>.
$$2\frac{4}{5} = \frac{14}{5} \text{ and } 3\frac{2}{3} = \frac{11}{3}$$

2) Find the reciprocal of $\frac{11}{3}$ and <u>multiply</u> as usual.
$$\frac{14}{5} \times \frac{3}{11} = \frac{14\times3}{5\times11} = \frac{42}{55}$$

Practice Questions

1) $\frac{3}{10} + \frac{4}{10}$ 2) a) $\frac{2}{3} - \frac{4}{9}$ b) $6 \times \frac{1}{12}$ (L2) 3) $\frac{7}{3} \div \frac{2}{9}$ (L3) 4) a) $4\frac{3}{5} \times 2\frac{1}{3}$ b) $\frac{59}{8} \div 6\frac{1}{2}$

Fractions

This is the final hurdle. The last page exclusively on fractions.
Just make sure you know your stuff by testing yourself on the questions below.

Finding a **Fraction of** Something

1) <u>Multiply</u> the 'something' by
   the <u>TOP</u> of the fraction...

2) ...then <u>divide</u> it by the <u>BOTTOM</u>.

> E.g. $\dfrac{9}{20}$ of £360 = £360 × 9 ÷ 20 = <u>£162</u>

Examples

John eats $\dfrac{2}{5}$ of a 500 g
bar of chocolate. How much
chocolate did he eat?

1) <u>Multiply</u> the   500 × 2 = 1000
   'something' by 2

2) Then <u>divide</u> by 5   1000 ÷ 5 = 200 g

Marcus has 324 songs on his laptop.
He deletes 1 out of every four of them.
How many songs did he have left?

1) Write 1 out of 4 as $\dfrac{1}{4}$
   a <u>fraction</u>.

2) <u>Multiply</u> by 1 and   324 × 1 ÷ 4 = 81
   divide by 4

3) <u>Subtract</u> from 324   324 − 81 = 243
   to find the number
   of songs <u>left</u>.

One Thing as a **Fraction of** Another

You can write one <u>number</u> as a fraction of <u>another number</u> just by putting the first number
over the second and <u>cancelling down</u>. This works if the first number is <u>bigger</u> than the
second number too — you'll just end up with a fraction <u>greater than 1</u>

> E.g. <u>132</u> as a fraction of 144 is $\dfrac{132}{144} = \dfrac{11}{12}$, and <u>144</u> as a fraction of 132 is $\dfrac{144}{132} = \dfrac{12}{11}$

Examples

Claire owns 64 books. 8 of them are fiction.
What fraction of her books are fiction?

1) Put the 8 <u>over</u> the 64 $\dfrac{8}{64}$

2) <u>Simplify</u> your answer. $\dfrac{8}{64} = \dfrac{1}{8}$

Write 30 cm as a fraction of 2 m.

1) Convert 2 m into cm
   so the measurements
   are in the same units.   2 m = 200 cm

2) Put the 30 <u>over</u> the 200 $\dfrac{30}{200}$

3) <u>Simplify</u> your answer. $\dfrac{30}{200} = \dfrac{3}{20}$

Practice Questions

1) Steph has 32 m of ribbon. She uses $\dfrac{3}{8}$ of it. How much did she use?

2) $\dfrac{5}{6}$ of the 354 Z-Factor contestants can't sing. How many contestants can't sing?

3) 12 out of 96 lions at Rugby Zoo like meat. What fraction of the lions dislike meat?

Percentage Basics

These simple percentage questions shouldn't give you much trouble. Especially if you remember:

> 1) '<u>Per cent</u>' means '<u>out of 100</u>', so 20% means '20 out of 100' = $\frac{20}{100}$
>
> 2) If a question asks you to work out the percentage <u>OF</u> something you can replace the word <u>OF</u> with a <u>multiplication</u> (×).

Find *x%* of *y*

Turn the percentage into a <u>decimal</u>, then <u>multiply</u>.

Examples

Find 18% of £4

1) Write 18% as a <u>decimal</u>:
   18% = 18 ÷ 100 = 0.18
2) <u>Multiply</u> 0.18 by £4:
   0.18 × £4 = £0.72

 Find 125% of 600 kg.

1) Write 125% as a <u>decimal</u>:
   125% = 125 ÷ 100 = 1.25
2) <u>Multiply</u> 1.25 by 600 kg:
   1.25 × 600 kg = 750 kg

Express *x* as a **Percentage** of *y*

<u>Divide</u> *x* by *y*, then multiply by <u>100</u>.

Example

Give 6p as a percentage of 96p.   <u>Divide</u> 6p by 96p, <u>then multiply</u> by 100:   (6 ÷ 96) × 100 = 6.25%

Example

Farmer Littlewood measured the width of his prized pumpkin at the start and end of the month. At the start of the month it was <u>90 cm</u> wide and at the end of the month it was <u>1.35 m</u> wide. Give the <u>width at the end</u> of the month <u>as a percentage</u> of the <u>width at the start</u>.

1) Make sure both amounts are in the <u>same units</u> — convert 1.35 m to cm.   1.35 m = 135 cm

2) <u>Divide</u> 135 cm by 90 cm, <u>then multiply</u> by 100:   (135 ÷ 90) × 100 = 150%

Compare Two Quantities Using **Percentages**

You can <u>compare</u> two <u>quantities</u> by <u>expressing</u> them both as <u>percentages</u>.

Example

Bottle A contains 350 ml of water and has a capacity of 500 ml. Bottle B contains 400 ml of water and has a capacity of 625 ml. **Which bottle is more full?**

1) Bottle A — (350 ÷ 500) × 100 = 70%

2) Bottle B — (400 ÷ 625) × 100 = 64%   70% is greater than 64% so **bottle A** is more full.

Practice Questions

1) Find: a) 39% of 505   b) 175% of 356
2) Give: a) 630 m as a percentage of 840 m   b) 1.2 km as a percentage of 750 m

Rounding Numbers and Estimating

You need to be able to use 3 different rounding methods.
We'll do decimal places first, but there's the same basic idea behind all three.

Decimal Places (d.p.)

To round to a given number of <u>decimal places</u>:

> *If you're rounding to 2 d.p. the last digit is the second digit after the decimal point.*

1) <u>Identify</u> the position of the '<u>last digit</u>' from the number of decimal places.

2) Then look at the next digit to the <u>right</u> — called <u>the decider</u>.

3) If the <u>decider</u> is <u>5 or more</u>, then <u>round up</u> the <u>last digit</u>.
    If the <u>decider</u> is <u>4 or less</u>, then leave the <u>last digit</u> as it is.

4) There must be <u>no more digits</u> after the last digit (not even zeros).

Example

What is 21.84 correct to <u>1 decimal place</u>?

$$21.\underset{\uparrow}{\textcircled{8}}\underset{\uparrow}{\textcircled{4}} = 21.\underset{\uparrow}{8}$$

<u>LAST DIGIT</u> to be written   <u>DECIDER</u>   The <u>LAST DIGIT</u> stays the <u>same</u>
(1st decimal place because   because the <u>DECIDER</u> is <u>4 or less</u>.
we're rounding to 1 d.p.)

Example

What is 39.7392739 to <u>2 decimal places</u>?

$$39 . 7\underset{\uparrow}{\textcircled{3}}\underset{\uparrow}{\textcircled{9}}2739 = 39.\underset{\uparrow}{74}$$

<u>LAST DIGIT</u> to be written   <u>DECIDER</u>   The <u>LAST DIGIT</u> rounds <u>UP</u>
(2nd decimal place because   because the <u>DECIDER</u> is <u>5 or more</u>.
we're rounding to 2 d.p.)

Watch Out for **Pesky Nines**

If you have to <u>round up</u> a <u>9</u> (to 10), replace the 9 with 0, and <u>add 1</u> to digit on the <u>left</u>.

Example

a) **Round 48.897 to 2.d.p.**

> *The question asks for 2 d.p. so you must put 48.90 not 48.9*

$$48.8\underset{\diagup \ \diagdown}{97} \longrightarrow 48.8\overset{9 \ 0}{\cancel{9}} \longrightarrow 48.90 \text{ to 2 d.p.}$$

<u>LAST DIGIT</u>   <u>DECIDER</u>

b) **Use a calculator to work out 638 ÷ (2 × 32). Round your answer to 1 d.p.**

$$638 \div (2 \times 32) = 9.96875 \longrightarrow \overset{10 \ \ 0}{9.\cancel{96}} \longrightarrow 10.0 \text{ to 1 d.p.}$$

Practice Questions

1) Give: a) 23.568 correct to 1 d.p.   b) 6.789 correct to 2 d.p.

2) Use a calculator to work out: a) 79 × (41 ÷ 24) to 1 d.p.   b) 377 ÷ (7 × 11) to 2 d.p.

Rounding Numbers and Estimating

To the **Nearest Whole Number**, **Ten**, **Hundred** etc.

You can round to the <u>nearest whole number</u>, <u>ten</u>, <u>tenth</u>, <u>hundred</u>, <u>thousandth</u> and so on.

1) <u>Identify the last digit</u>, e.g. for the nearest <u>whole number</u> it's the <u>ones</u> position.

2) <u>Round the last digit</u> and <u>fill in with zeros</u> up to the decimal point.

Example

Round 61 729 to the nearest <u>thousand</u>.

<u>LAST DIGIT</u> is in the 'thousands' position.   Fill in <u>3 zeros</u> up to decimal point.

$$6\textcircled{1}729 = 62000$$

<u>DECIDER</u> is 5 or more. ⟹ Last digit <u>rounds up</u>.

Significant Figures (s.f.)

The <u>1st significant figure</u> of any number is <u>the first digit which isn't a zero</u>.

The <u>2nd, 3rd, etc. significant figures</u> follow straight after the 1st — they're allowed to be zeros.

To <u>round</u> to a given number of significant figures:

1) Find the <u>last digit</u> — e.g. for 3 s.f., it's the 3rd <u>significant figure</u>.

2) Use the digit to the right of it as the <u>decider</u>, just like for d.p.

3) Once you've rounded, <u>fill up</u> with <u>zeros</u>, up to but <u>not beyond</u> the decimal point.

$$0.00230$$

S.F: 1st 2nd 3rd

Example

Round 1276.7 to <u>3 significant figures</u>.

<u>LAST DIGIT</u> is the 3rd sig. fig.

Need a <u>zero</u> to fill up to decimal point.

$$12\textcircled{7}6.7 = 1280$$

<u>DECIDER</u> is 5 or more. ⟹ Last digit <u>rounds up</u>.

Estimating

Estimating can help you to work out a <u>rough answer</u> or <u>check</u> your answer is roughly correct.

You should round to 1 significant figure if you've not been told.

<u>Round everything off</u> to <u>nice convenient numbers</u> and then work out the answer.

Example

Estimate $\dfrac{63.26 \times 116.2}{1.89}$ by rounding each number to 1 s.f.

— means 'approximately equal to'.

<u>Round</u> each number to <u>1 s.f</u> and do the calculation with the rounded numbers.

$$\dfrac{63.26 \times 116.2}{1.89} \approx \dfrac{60 \times 100}{2} = \dfrac{6000}{2} = 3000$$

Practice Questions

1) Round: a) 17.548 to the nearest whole number.   b) 0.256 to 2 s.f.

2) Estimate 215 × 1.89   3) Estimate 17.3 × 31.87 by rounding each number to 1 s.f.

Powers and Roots

They may look small, but they're quite mighty. Take a look at these powers and roots.

Powers *are Useful Shorthand*

$2^3 = 2 \times 2 \times 2$ $2^5 = 2 \times 2 \times 2 \times 2 \times 2$

1) Powers tell you how many of the same number are multiplied together, e.g. $3^4 = 3 \times 3 \times 3 \times 3$

$2^2 = 4$	$2^3 = 8$	$2^4 = 16$	$2^5 = 32$

2) Find powers using your calculator by pressing the $x^\blacksquare$ key. E.g. $\boxed{9}\ \boxed{x^\blacksquare}\ \boxed{4}\ \boxed{=}$ gives $9^4 = 6561$

$3^2 = 9$	$3^3 = 27$	$3^4 = 81$	$3^5 = 243$

3) Anything to the <u>power 1</u> is <u>itself</u>, e.g. $4^1 = 4$

$4^2 = 16$	$4^3 = 64$	$4^4 = 256$	$4^5 = 1024$

4) Anything to the <u>power 0</u> is <u>1</u>, e.g. $12^0 = 1$

$5^2 = 25$	$5^3 = 125$	$5^4 = 625$	$5^5 = 3125$

Square *Roots*

'<u>Squared</u>' means '<u>multiplied by itself</u>': $6^2 = 6 \times 6 = 36$

<u>SQUARE ROOT</u> $\sqrt{}$ is the <u>reverse process</u>: $\sqrt{36} = 6$

'Square Root' means 'What number **times by itself** gives...'

Examples

What is $\sqrt{81}$?

9 times itself gives 81 $81 = 9 \times 9$ So $\sqrt{81} = 9$

What is $\sqrt{7.84}$?

Press: $\boxed{\sqrt{}}\ \boxed{7.84}\ \boxed{=}$ 2.8

Find both square roots of 100

$10 \times 10 = 100$
$-10 \times -10 = 100$
so $\sqrt{100} = 10$ and -10

All numbers also have a negative square root — it's just the '–' version of the normal positive one.

Cube *Roots*

'<u>Cubed</u>' means '<u>multiplied by itself and then by itself again</u>': $2^3 = 2 \times 2 \times 2 = 8$

<u>CUBE ROOT</u> $\sqrt[3]{}$ is the <u>reverse process</u>: $\sqrt[3]{8} = 2$

'Cube Root' means 'What number **times by itself** and then by **itself again** gives...'

Examples

What is $\sqrt[3]{27}$?

3 times itself and then by itself again gives 27 $27 = 3 \times 3 \times 3$ So $\sqrt[3]{27} = 3$

Unlike square roots there is only one answer.

What is $\sqrt[3]{4913}$?

Press: $\boxed{\sqrt[3]{}}\ \boxed{4913}\ \boxed{=}$ 17

Roots *aren't always* Exact

Sometimes a number can only be given <u>exactly</u> using a $\sqrt{}$ sign.
For example, $\sqrt{2} = 1.41421...$ can be <u>rounded</u> to <u>1.4</u> but $1.4^2 = 1.96$, <u>not 2</u>.
So, if you're asked for an <u>exact</u> answer you'll need to write $\sqrt{2}$.

Practice Questions

1) Write down all the square and cube numbers between 3 and 99

2) Calculate: a) $9^2 + 1^4$ b) the square root of 121   c) the cube root of 512

Standard Form

Standard form (or 'standard index form') is useful for writing <u>very big</u> or <u>very small</u> numbers in a more convenient way. A number written in standard form must <u>always</u> be in <u>exactly</u> this form:

This <u>number</u> must <u>always</u> be <u>between 1 and 10</u>.
(The fancy way of saying this is $1 \leq A < 10$)

$$A \times 10^n$$

This number is just the <u>number of places</u> the <u>decimal point</u> moves.

Three Rules for Standard Form

1) The <u>front number</u> must always be between <u>1 and 10</u>.

2) The power of 10, n, is <u>how far the decimal point moves</u>.

3) n is <u>positive</u> for <u>big</u> numbers, n is <u>negative</u> for <u>small</u> numbers.

Three *Important* Examples

Example

Express 259 000 in standard form.

1) <u>Move the decimal point</u> until 259 000 becomes 2.59 ($1 \leq A < 10$).

2) The decimal point has moved <u>5 places</u> so $n = 5$, giving: 10^5.

3) 259 000 is a <u>big number</u> so n is +5, not –5.

$$= 2.59 \times 10^5$$

Example

Express 0.0035 in standard form.

1) The decimal point must move <u>3 places</u> to give 3.5 ($1 \leq A < 10$). So the power of 10 is 3.

2) Since 0.0035 is a <u>small number</u> it must be 10^{-3}, not 10^{+3}.

$$= 3.5 \times 10^{-3}$$

Example

Write these numbers in order from smallest to largest:

2.25×10^4 7.98×10^{-4} 6880 3.12×10^4 6.75×10^3 0.000134

1) First <u>convert</u> all the numbers into standard form.
$6880 = 6.88 \times 10^3$ $0.000134 = 1.34 \times 10^{-4}$

2) Now <u>group</u> the numbers with the <u>same power</u> together and order them based on the power.
7.98×10^{-4} 1.34×10^{-4} 6.88×10^3 6.75×10^3 2.25×10^4 3.12×10^4

3) Finally <u>order each group</u> by the <u>size</u> of the <u>front number</u> — give the numbers in the form they are given in the question.
0.000134 7.98×10^{-4} 6.75×10^3 6880 2.25×10^4 3.12×10^4

Practice Question

1) Express these numbers in standard form: a) 19 000 000   b) 0.0000796

Summary Questions

Well, that's <u>section 1</u> done — have a go at these questions to see how much you can remember.
- Try these questions and <u>tick off each one</u> when you <u>get it right</u>.
- When you've done <u>all the questions</u> for a topic and are <u>completely happy</u> with it, tick off the topic.

Only use your calculator when the question tells you to.

(L1) <u>Ordering Numbers and Calculations (p3-13)</u> ☐

1) Find the value of: a) $4 + 10 \div 2$ b) $12 \div 3 \times 2$ c) $(8 \times 5) \div 20$ ☑
2) Work out the following by dividing by factors: a) $270 \div 18$ b) $210 \div 35$ ☑
3) Put these numbers in ascending order: 0.02, 54, –11.8, 23.91, –0.09, 0.001, –0.51, 0.9 ☐
4) On Day 1 it was –6 °C, Day 2 was –8 °C and Day 3 was –7.5 °C. Which day was coldest? ☐
5) Work out: a) $417 + 194$ b) $753 - 157$ c) $(2.3 + 1.123) - 0.75$ ☐
6) Find: a) 1.223×100 b) 15.12×1000 c) $6.75 \div 10$ d) $1.24 \div 200$ ☐
7) Work out: a) 131×19 b) $672 \div 14$ c) 9.12×34 d) $65.65 \div 13$ ☑

(L1) <u>Types of Number, Factors and Multiples (p14-17)</u> ☐

8) Work out: a) $-8 + 6$ b) $-4 - 10$ c) -7×-8 d) $81 \div -9$ ☑
9) Find all the prime numbers between: a) 40 and 50   b) 80 and 90 ☑
10) Find: a) the first 5 multiples of 13   b) all the factors of 36 ☑
11) Express 252 as the product of prime factors. ☑
12) Find the highest number that divides both 28 and 40 ☑

(L1) <u>Fractions, Decimals and Percentages (p18-22)</u> ☐

13) Write: a) 0.6 as a fraction and a percentage   b) 65% as a fraction and a decimal ☑
14) a) Give two fractions equivalent to $\frac{3}{5}$ b) Which is bigger, 60% of 880 or $\frac{4}{5}$ of 640? ☐
15) Work out: a) $\frac{2}{8} + \frac{3}{8}$ b) $\frac{4}{5} - \frac{2}{5}$ c) $\frac{1}{9} + \frac{4}{9}$ ☑
16) Simplify: a) $\frac{1}{3} + \frac{5}{9}$ b) $\frac{7}{10} - \frac{1}{2}$ (L2) c) $\frac{7}{10} \times \frac{5}{6}$ d) $\frac{2}{11} \div \frac{3}{10}$ ☑
17) Simplify: a) $\frac{4}{9} + 1\frac{1}{3}$ b) $2\frac{1}{4} - \frac{5}{8}$ (L3) c) $4\frac{1}{2} \times 2\frac{1}{4}$ d) $3\frac{2}{3} \div -\frac{1}{6}$ ☑
18) Calculate: a) $\frac{2}{9}$ of 540   b) $\frac{3}{7}$ of 490   c) 15% of 78   (L2) d) 180% of £95 ☑
19) Use a calculator to give: a) 7 as a fraction of 182   b) 61p as a percentage of £15.25 ☑

(L1) <u>Rounding and Estimating (p23-24)</u> ☐

20) Round: a) 164.353 to 1 d.p.   b) 765 444 to the nearest ten ☑
21) Estimate the value of: a) $\frac{20.5 \times 4.9}{9.7}$ b) $\frac{498 \times 98}{53}$ ☑
(L2) 22) a) Round 76 233 to 2 s.f.   b) Estimate 22.2×50.3 by rounding each number to 1 s.f. ☑

(L1) <u>Powers, Roots and Standard Form (p25-26)</u> ☐

23) Which of these numbers are square numbers?   16   38   44   49   121   125 ☐
24) Use a calculator to find: a) $\sqrt{249.64}$ (L2) b) $\sqrt[3]{2744}$ ☑
(L3) 25) Express: a) 2×10^8 as an ordinary number   b) 0.00044 in standard form ☑
(L3) 26) Which of these numbers is the smallest?   0.00005 1.7×10^{-5} 9.8×10^{-4} 0.00072 ☑

Algebra — Simplifying Terms

Make sure you understand and learn these basic rules for dealing with algebraic expressions.

Terms

Before you can do anything else with algebra, you must understand what a <u>term</u> is:

> ### A TERM IS EITHER A NUMBER, A LETTER OR COLLECTION OF NUMBERS OR LETTERS MULTIPLIED/DIVIDED TOGETHER

Terms are separated by <u>+ and – signs</u>. Every term has a + or – attached to the <u>front of it</u>.

If there's no sign in front of the first term, it means there's an invisible + sign.

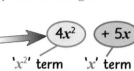 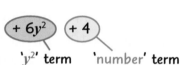

'x^2' **term**   'x' **term**   'y' **term**   'y^2' **term**   'number' **term**

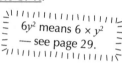

$6y^2$ means $6 \times y^2$ — see page 29.

Simplifying or 'Collecting Like Terms'

To <u>simplify</u> an algebraic expression made up of all the <u>same terms</u>, just <u>add</u> or <u>subtract</u> them.

— **Examples** —

Simplify $r + r + r + r$

Just <u>add up</u> all the r's:

$r + r + r + r = 4r$

'r' just means '$1r$'.

Simplify $2s + 3s - s$

Again, just <u>combine the terms</u> — don't forget there's a '–' before the last s:

$2s + 3s - s = 4s$

To <u>simplify</u> an algebraic expression with a mixture of <u>different letters</u> and <u>numbers</u>, you combine '<u>like terms</u>' (e.g. all the x terms, all the y terms, all the number terms, etc.).

— **Example** —

Simplify $7x + 3 - x - 2$

Invisible + sign ———

x-terms   number terms

$(7x) \ (+3) \ (-x) \ (-2) = (+7x) \ (-x) \ (+3) \ (-2) = 6x + 1$

$\qquad\qquad\qquad\qquad\qquad\qquad 6x \qquad +1$

1) Put <u>bubbles</u> round each term — be sure you capture the ± or – sign in front of each.
2) Then you can move the bubbles into the <u>best order</u> so that <u>like terms</u> are together.
3) <u>Combine like terms</u>.

Negative Numbers

The negative number rules from page 14 also apply to algebra — so make sure you learn them.

+	+	makes	+
+	–	makes	–
–	+	makes	–
–	–	makes	+

Use these rules when:

1) <u>Multiplying or dividing</u>.
2) <u>Two signs are together</u>.

E.g. $-2 \times 3 = -6$, $-4p \div -2 = +2p$

E.g. $5 - -4 = 5 + 4 = 9$, $-x + -y = -x - y$

Practice Questions

1) Simplify a) $a + a + a$ b) $3d + 7d - 2d$ c) $8x - y - 2x + 3y$
2) Simplify a) $-3 \times 4f$ b) $-5x \times -5$ c) $3a - -b$

Algebra — Simplifying Terms

On this page we'll look at some rules that will help you simplify expressions that have letters and numbers multiplied together.

Letters **Multiplied** Together

Watch out for these combinations of letters in algebra that regularly catch people out:

1) abc means $a \times b \times c$ and $3a$ means $3 \times a$. The ×'s are often left out to make it clearer.

2) gn^2 means $g \times n \times n$. Note that only the n is squared, not the g as well.

3) $(gn)^2$ means $g \times g \times n \times n$. The brackets mean that <u>BOTH</u> letters are squared.

4) <u>Powers</u> tell you <u>how many</u> letters are multiplied together — so $r^6 = r \times r \times r \times r \times r \times r$.

Careful — h multiplied by itself then by itself again is h^3, <u>not</u> 3h. (3h means h + h + h or 3 × h).

> **Examples**
>
> **Simplify $h \times h \times h$**
>
> You have 3 h's <u>multiplied together</u>:
>
> $h \times h \times h = h^3$
>
> **Simplify $3r \times 2s \times 2$**
>
> Multiply the <u>numbers</u> together, then the <u>letters</u> together:
>
> $3r \times 2s \times 2$
> $= 3 \times 2 \times 2 \times r \times s = 12rs$

Power Rules in Algebra

You can use these <u>power rules</u> on <u>algebraic expressions</u>:

1) When <u>multiplying</u>, you <u>add</u> the powers.   2) When <u>dividing</u>, you <u>subtract</u> the powers.

3) When doing a <u>power to a power</u>, you <u>multiply</u> the powers.

> **Examples**
>
> **Simplify $n^5 \times n^2$**
>
> You're multiplying, so <u>add</u> the powers:
>
> $n^5 \times n^2 = n^{5+2} = n^7$
>
> **Simplify $m^{13} \div m^5$**
>
> You're dividing, so <u>subtract</u> the powers:
>
> $m^{13} \div m^5 = m^{13-5} = m^8$
>
> **Simplify $(s^2)^5$**
>
> You're doing power to a power, so <u>multiply</u> the powers:
>
> $(s^2)^5 = s^{2 \times 5} = s^{10}$

Algebraic **Fractions**

If you have a <u>fraction</u> with letters and numbers, then you might be able to <u>simplify</u>. Just do it the same way you would with a normal fraction.

In equations, the number written before a letter is called the <u>coefficient</u>. You should write it as a whole number or a fraction.

> **Examples**
>
> **Simplify $\dfrac{5r}{20}$**
>
> Divide the top and bottom by 5:
>
>
>
> $\dfrac{5r}{20} = \dfrac{r}{4}$
>
> (L3) **Simplify $\dfrac{7e}{e}$**
>
> Divide the top and bottom by e:
>
>
>
> $\dfrac{7e}{e} = \dfrac{7}{1} = 7$

Practice Questions

1) Simplify   a) $d \times d \times d \times d \times d$ b) $2e \times 8f$ c) $p^6 \times p^4$ d) $\dfrac{8j}{2}$

(L3) 2) Simplify   a) $\dfrac{4m}{m}$ b) $\dfrac{20f}{2f}$ c) $\dfrac{15c^3}{5c}$ d) $\dfrac{(2ef^3)^2}{f^2}$

Algebra — Multiplying Out Brackets

Multiplying out brackets (also called 'expanding brackets') can be a bit tough.
No need to panic though — here's how it's done.

Multiplying by a **Number**

1) The number <u>outside</u> the brackets multiplies <u>each separate term</u> inside the brackets.

2) A minus <u>outside</u> the brackets <u>reverses</u> all the signs <u>inside</u> the brackets when you multiply.

Examples

Expand $3(x + 1)$.

Just multiply 3 by x, then 3 by 1

$3(x + 1) = (3 \times x) + (3 \times 1)$
$= 3x + 3$

Expand $-2(4y - 5)$.

<u>Multiply</u> -2 by $4y$
then -2 by -5

$-2(4y - 5)$

Two negatives make a positive (p.28).

$= (-2 \times 4y) + (-2 \times -5)$
$= -8y + 10$

Multiplying by a **Letter**

This is basically the same as multiplying by a <u>number</u>. Remember, when <u>letters</u>
are multiplied together, they are just written <u>next to</u> each other, e.g. $p \times q = pq$ (page 29).

Examples

 Expand $a(b + 2)$.

Multiply a by b, then a by 2

$a(b + 2) = (a \times b) + (a \times 2)$
$= ab + 2a$

 Expand $3cd(5e - 2f)$.

<u>Multiply</u> $3cd$ by $5e$, then $3cd$ by $-2f$.

$3cd(5e - 2f) = (3cd \times 5e) + (3cd \times -2f)$
$= 15cde - 6cdf$

Multiplying to get **Powers**

1) If the letter outside the bracket is the same as a letter inside, then you'll end up with a <u>power</u>.
2) Remember, $a \times a = a^2$, and xy^2 means $x \times y \times y$, but $(xy)^2$ means $x \times x \times y \times y$ (see p.29).

Examples

 Expand $y(y + 5)$.

Multiply y by y, then y by 5

$y(y + 5) = (y \times y) + (y \times 5)$
$= y^2 + 5y$

 Expand $-r^2(2r - 7s)$.

<u>Multiply</u> $-r^2$ by $2r$, then $-r^2$ by $-7s$.

$-r^2(2r - 7s)$

$r^2 \times s = r^2s$

$= (-r^2 \times 2r) + (-r^2 \times -7s)$
$= -2r^3 + 7r^2s$

Practice Questions

1) Expand: a) $2(4 - x)$ b) $6(2x - 3y)$
2) Expand and simplify: $5 - 2(x + 2)$
 3) Expand: a) $h(8 - d)$ b) $2j(3 - j)$ c) $3b^2(a - 2b)$

Algebra — Taking Out Common Factors

Now you know how to expand brackets, it's time to put them back in. This is called factorising. Follow these three rules and you can't go wrong:

> 1) Take out the <u>biggest common factor</u> that goes into all the terms.
> 2) Open the brackets and fill in all the bits needed to <u>reproduce each term</u>.
> 3) <u>Check</u> your answer by <u>multiplying out</u> the brackets again.

*Taking Out a **Number***

This is the <u>exact reverse</u> of multiplying out brackets. Look for a <u>common factor</u> of the numbers in both terms and take it <u>outside</u> the brackets. The biggest common factor is the <u>biggest number</u> that the numbers in <u>both terms</u> divide by.

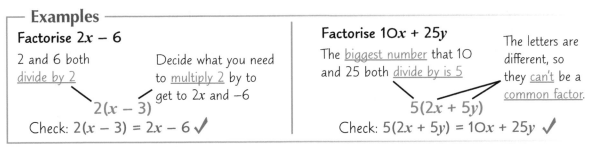

— **Examples** —

Factorise $2x - 6$

2 and 6 both <u>divide by 2</u>

Decide what you need to <u>multiply 2</u> by to get to $2x$ and -6

$2(x - 3)$

Check: $2(x - 3) = 2x - 6$ ✓

Factorise $10x + 25y$

The <u>biggest number</u> that 10 and 25 both <u>divide by is 5</u>

The letters are different, so they <u>can't</u> be a <u>common factor</u>.

$5(2x + 5y)$

Check: $5(2x + 5y) = 10x + 25y$ ✓

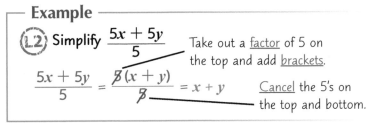

— **Example** —

(L2) Simplify $\dfrac{5x + 5y}{5}$ Take out a <u>factor</u> of 5 on the top and add <u>brackets</u>.

$\dfrac{5x + 5y}{5} = \dfrac{\cancel{5}(x + y)}{\cancel{5}} = x + y$ <u>Cancel</u> the 5's on the top and bottom.

*Taking Out a **Letter*** (L3)

If the <u>same letter</u> appears in <u>all</u> the terms (but to <u>different powers</u>), you can take out some <u>power</u> of the <u>letter</u> as a <u>common factor</u>. You might be able to take out a <u>number</u> as well.

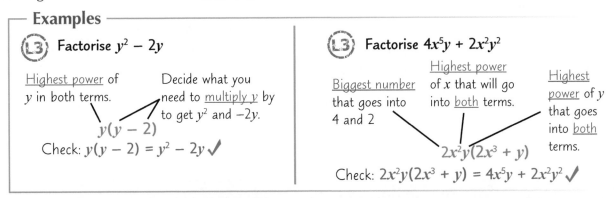

— **Examples** —

(L3) Factorise $y^2 - 2y$

<u>Highest power</u> of y in both terms.

Decide what you need to <u>multiply y</u> by to get y^2 and $-2y$.

$y(y - 2)$

Check: $y(y - 2) = y^2 - 2y$ ✓

(L3) Factorise $4x^5y + 2x^2y^2$

<u>Biggest number</u> that goes into 4 and 2

<u>Highest power</u> of x that will go into <u>both</u> terms.

<u>Highest power</u> of y that goes into <u>both</u> terms.

$2x^2y(2x^3 + y)$

Check: $2x^2y(2x^3 + y) = 4x^5y + 2x^2y^2$ ✓

Practice Questions

1) Factorise: a) $4 - 10r$ b) $6x + 2y$

2) Factorise fully: a) $30s + 12$ b) $-40 - 24t$ c) $-4m - 8n$

(L3) 3) Factorise fully: a) $a^2 + 4a$ b) $9b^2 - 3b$ c) $9c^2d + 12cd^3$

Solving Equations

To solve equations, you must find the value of *x* (or any given letter) that makes the equation true.
To find this value of *x*, rearrange the equation until you end up with '*x* = ' on one side.
Here are a few important points to remember when rearranging.

Golden Rules
1) Always do the <u>SAME thing</u> to <u>both sides of the equation</u>.
2) To get rid of something, do the <u>opposite</u>.
   The opposite of + is − and the opposite of − is +.
   The opposite of × is ÷ and the opposite of ÷ is ×.
3) Keep going until you have a letter <u>on its own</u>.

Solving **One-Step** Equations

One-step equations are exactly what they say on the tin — one step and you're done.

Examples

Solve $x + 3 = 7$

| The opposite of + 3 is − 3 |

$x + 3 = 7$

This means 'take away 3 from both sides'.

$(− 3)\quad x + 3 − 3 = 7 − 3$

$x = 4$

Solve $x − 2 = 3$

| The opposite of − 2 is + 2 |

$x − 2 = 3$

$(+ 2)\quad x − 2 + 2 = 3 + 2$

$x = 5$

Examples

Solve $2x = 10$

| 2x means 2 × x, so do the opposite — divide both sides by 2 |

$2x = 10$

$(÷ 2)\quad 2x ÷ 2 = 10 ÷ 2$

$x = 5$

Solve $\frac{x}{2} = 4$

| $\frac{x}{2}$ means x ÷ 2, so do the opposite — multiply both sides by 2 |

$\frac{x}{2} = 4$

$(× 2)\quad \frac{x}{2} × 2 = 4 × 2$

$x = 8$

Solving **Two-Step** Equations

If you come across an equation like $8x − 2 = 14$ (where there's an <u>x-term</u> and a <u>number</u> on the <u>same side</u>), use the methods above to solve it — just do it in <u>two steps</u>:
1) <u>Add or subtract</u> the number first.   2) <u>Multiply or divide</u> to get '*x* = '.

Examples

Solve $5x + 2 = 12$

$5x + 2 = 12$

| The opposite of + 2 is − 2 |

$(− 2)\quad 5x + 2 − 2 = 12 − 2$

$5x = 10$

| The opposite of × 5 is ÷ 5 |

$(÷ 5)\quad 5x ÷ 5 = 10 ÷ 5$

$x = 2$

(L2) Solve $−8 = 3x − 6$

$−8 = 3x − 6$

| The opposite of − 6 is + 6 |

$(+ 6)\quad −8 + 6 = 3x − 6 + 6$

$−2 = 3x$

| The opposite of × 3 is ÷ 3 |

$(÷ 3)\quad −2 ÷ 3 = 3x ÷ 3$

$−\frac{2}{3} = x$, so $x = −\frac{2}{3}$

Practice Questions

It's a good idea to write down what you're doing at every stage in brackets. Try it out:

1) Solve these equations: a) $x + 6 = 9$ b) $x − 2 = 9$ c) $9x = 27$ d) $\frac{x}{3} = 7$

(L2) 2) Solve these equations: a) $8 = 4x + 5$ b) $−2 = 3x − 7$

(L2) 3) Solve these equations: a) $\frac{x}{2} − 3 = 7$ b) $2 − 7x = −5$

Solving Equations

You're not done with solving equations yet — not by a long shot. This is where it gets really fun.

Equations with an 'x' on **Both Sides**

For equations like $3x + 1 = x - 7$ (where there's an x-term on <u>each side</u>), you have to:

1) Get all the x's on one side and all the <u>numbers</u> on the other.
2) <u>Multiply or divide</u> to get '$x =$'.

The letters in an equation might not always be x. They could be any letter.

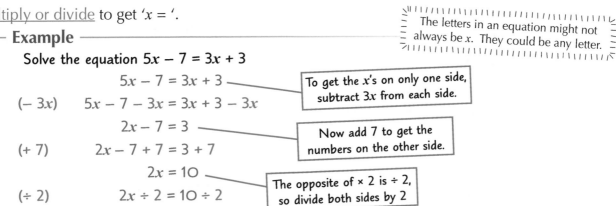

Example

Solve the equation $5x - 7 = 3x + 3$

$$5x - 7 = 3x + 3$$

$(-3x)$ $5x - 7 - 3x = 3x + 3 - 3x$ To get the x's on only one side, subtract $3x$ from each side.

$$2x - 7 = 3$$

$(+7)$ $2x - 7 + 7 = 3 + 7$ Now add 7 to get the numbers on the other side.

$$2x = 10$$

$(÷2)$ $2x ÷ 2 = 10 ÷ 2$ The opposite of × 2 is ÷ 2, so divide both sides by 2.

$$x = 5$$

Equations with **Brackets**

If the equation has <u>brackets</u> in, you have to <u>multiply out</u> the brackets before solving it as above.

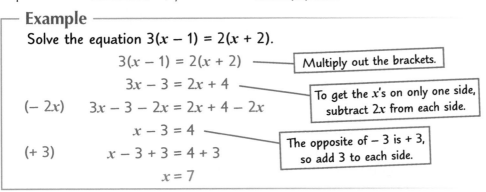

Example

Solve the equation $3(x - 1) = 2(x + 2)$.

$$3(x - 1) = 2(x + 2)$$ Multiply out the brackets.

$$3x - 3 = 2x + 4$$

$(-2x)$ $3x - 3 - 2x = 2x + 4 - 2x$ To get the x's on only one side, subtract $2x$ from each side.

$$x - 3 = 4$$

$(+3)$ $x - 3 + 3 = 4 + 3$ The opposite of − 3 is + 3, so add 3 to each side.

$$x = 7$$

Example

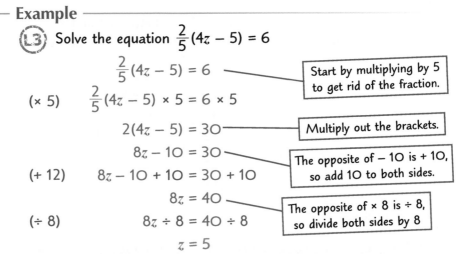

(L3) Solve the equation $\frac{2}{5}(4z - 5) = 6$

$$\frac{2}{5}(4z - 5) = 6$$ Start by multiplying by 5 to get rid of the fraction.

$(× 5)$ $\frac{2}{5}(4z - 5) × 5 = 6 × 5$

$$2(4z - 5) = 30$$ Multiply out the brackets.

$$8z - 10 = 30$$ The opposite of − 10 is + 10, so add 10 to both sides.

$(+12)$ $8z - 10 + 10 = 30 + 10$

$$8z = 40$$ The opposite of × 8 is ÷ 8, so divide both sides by 8.

$(÷8)$ $8z ÷ 8 = 40 ÷ 8$

$$z = 5$$

Practice Questions

1) Solve $3x - 5 = 4x + 5$ 2) Solve $2(2x - 3) = 6(x - 2)$ (L3) 3) Solve $\frac{1}{3}(3x - 5) = 1$

Solving Equations

Solving Simple Quadratic Equations

The <u>nastiest equation</u> you can expect in the exam is one with x^2 in it. If you end up with 'x^2 = a number' you can solve it by taking the <u>square roots</u> of each side. Remember that when you take the square root of a number the answer can be <u>positive</u> or <u>negative</u>.

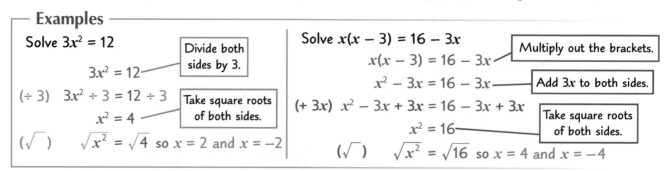

Examples

Solve $3x^2 = 12$

$$3x^2 = 12$$ — Divide both sides by 3.

$(\div 3)$ $3x^2 \div 3 = 12 \div 3$ — Take square roots of both sides.

$$x^2 = 4$$

$(\sqrt{\ })$ $\sqrt{x^2} = \sqrt{4}$ so $x = 2$ and $x = -2$

Solve $x(x - 3) = 16 - 3x$

$$x(x - 3) = 16 - 3x$$ — Multiply out the brackets.

$$x^2 - 3x = 16 - 3x$$ — Add $3x$ to both sides.

$(+ 3x)$ $x^2 - 3x + 3x = 16 - 3x + 3x$ — Take square roots of both sides.

$$x^2 = 16$$

$(\sqrt{\ })$ $\sqrt{x^2} = \sqrt{16}$ so $x = 4$ and $x = -4$

Trial and Improvement can help to solve Harder Equations

The basic idea of trial and improvement is to keep trying <u>different values</u> of x that are getting <u>closer</u> and <u>closer</u> to the solution. Here's the <u>method</u> to follow:

STEP 1: Put <u>2 values</u> into the equation that give <u>opposite cases</u> (one too big, one too small).

STEP 2: Next choose a value <u>between</u> the two opposite cases and put it into the equation.

STEP 3: Repeat STEP 2 until

EITHER you have an exact solution — then you're done.
OR you have <u>two numbers</u>:
 • both to 1 d.p.
 • <u>differing by 1</u> in the last digit (e.g. 4.3 and 4.4).
These are the <u>two possible answers</u>.

If you had to find an approximate solution to 2 d.p., the method is just the same — except you carry on until you end up with 2 numbers to 2 d.p. instead of 1 d.p.

STEP 4: Try the <u>exact middle value</u> of the two possible answers to decide which one it is.

It's a good idea to keep track of your working in a <u>table</u> — see the example below.
Make sure you show <u>all your working</u>, so the examiner can see what method you've used.

Example

A solution to the equation $5x^2 + 2x = 20$ lies between 1 and 2
Use trial and improvement to find the solution to this equation to 1 d.p.

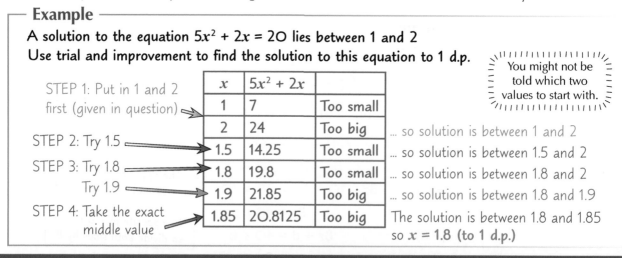

STEP 1: Put in 1 and 2 first (given in question)

STEP 2: Try 1.5

STEP 3: Try 1.8
Try 1.9

STEP 4: Take the exact middle value

You might not be told which two values to start with.

x	$5x^2 + 2x$		
1	7	Too small	
2	24	Too big	... so solution is between 1 and 2
1.5	14.25	Too small	... so solution is between 1.5 and 2
1.8	19.8	Too small	... so solution is between 1.8 and 2
1.9	21.85	Too big	... so solution is between 1.8 and 1.9
1.85	20.8125	Too big	The solution is between 1.8 and 1.85 so $x = 1.8$ (to 1 d.p.)

Practice Questions

1) Solve these equations: a) $x^2 = 9$ b) $x^2 + 5 = 30$ c) $x(2x + 1) = x + 2$

2) A solution to $8x^2 + 4x = 8$ lies between 0 and 1.
   Use trial sind improvement to find the solution to this equation to 1 d.p.

Using Expressions and Formulas

Expressions and formulas will come up again and again in your exams, so make sure you're happy with using them. The first thing you need to be able to do is simple — just put numbers into them.

Substitute **Numbers** for **Letters**

You might be given an <u>expression</u> or <u>formula</u> and asked to work out its <u>value</u> when you put in <u>certain numbers</u>. All you have to do here is follow this <u>method</u>.

1) Write out the <u>expression</u> or formula.
2) Write it <u>again</u>, directly underneath, but <u>substituting numbers for letters</u>.
3) Work it out <u>in stages</u>. Use <u>BODMAS</u> (see p.3) to work things out in the <u>right order</u>. <u>Write down</u> values for each bit as you go along.
4) <u>DO NOT</u> attempt to do it <u>all in one go</u> on your calculator — you're more likely to make <u>mistakes</u>.

Example

Find the value of $3j - 2k$ when $j = 4$ and $k = 5$

$3j - 2k$ ———————— 1) Write out the <u>expression</u>.

$= 3 \times 4 - 2 \times 5$ —— 2) Write it <u>again</u>, <u>substituting numbers for letters</u>.

$= 12 - 10$ ———————— 3) Work out the <u>multiplications</u> first, then do the <u>subtraction</u>.

$= 2$

Example

The formula for finding the density in g/cm³ (**D**), of an object given its mass in g (**M**), and volume in cm³ (**V**), is $D = \dfrac{M}{V}$. Find **D** when $M = 72$ and $V = 8$.

$D = \dfrac{M}{V}$ ————————————— 1) Write out the <u>formula</u>.

$D = \dfrac{72}{8}$ ————————————— 2) Write it <u>again</u>, <u>substituting numbers for letters</u>.

$D = 9$ so the density is 9 g/cm³. —— 3) Work out the <u>division</u>.

Sometimes you might need to do a bit of <u>solving</u> to get your answer.
<u>Substitute</u> the numbers in <u>first</u>, and then solve as usual.

Example

A formula used in physics is $s = vt - \dfrac{1}{2}at^2$.
Work out the value of v if $s = 10$, $t = 5$ and $a = 4$

$s = vt - \dfrac{1}{2}at^2$ ————————

$10 = (v \times 5) - (\dfrac{1}{2} \times 4 \times 5 \times 5)$ ——— 1) Write out the <u>formula</u>.
2) Write it <u>again</u>, substituting numbers for letters.

$10 = 5v - 50$

(+ 50) $10 + 50 = 5v - 50 + 50$ ———— 3) <u>Solve</u> to find v.

(÷ 5) $60 \div 5 = 5v \div 5$

$12 = v$, or $v = 12$

Practice Questions

1) $C = 5a + 2b$. Find the value of C when $a = 8$, $b = 3$

2) Find the value of z in $z + xy = y^2$ when $x = 7$ and $y = 2$

Making Formulas from Words

Before getting started on formulas, make sure you can remember these definitions.

EXPRESSION — a collection of terms (see p.28). Expressions DON'T have an = sign in them.
EQUATION — an expression with an = sign in it (so you can solve it).
FORMULA — a rule that helps you work something out (it will also have an = sign in it).

Making a Formula from Given Information

Making formulas from words can be a bit confusing as you're given a lot of information in one go.
You just have to go through it slowly and carefully and extract the maths from it.

Example

Ruby is x years old. Alia is 3 years older than Ruby.
Jeremy is 5 times as old as Ruby.

a) Write an expression for Alia's age in terms of x.

Alia is 3 years older, so add 3

Ruby's age is x
So Alia's age is $x + 3$

b) Write an expression for Jeremy's age in terms of x.

5 times older

Ruby's age is x
So Jeremy's age is $5 \times x = 5x$

Example

The cooking time (T minutes) for a turkey is 40 minutes per kilogram (k),
plus an extra 20 minutes. Write a formula for T in terms of k.

$$T = 40k + 20$$

A turkey with mass k will take $40 \times k$ minutes

Don't forget to add on the extra time (20 minutes)

Because you're asked for a formula, you must include the '$T =$' bit (i.e. don't just put $40k + 20$).

Using Your Formula to Solve Problems

Sometimes, you might be asked to write a formula and use it to solve a problem.

Example

A mechanic charges £100 plus £50 for each part he replaces (R). Si gets a repair bill of £450
Write a formula for the total repair cost and use it to find how many parts were replaced on Si's car.

Each part (R) costs £50

total repair cost = $50R + 100$

Don't forget to add on the £100 fixed charge.

$$450 = 50R + 100$$
$$(-100) \quad 450 - 100 = 50R + 100 - 100$$
$$350 = 50R$$
$$(\div 50) \quad 350 \div 50 = 50R \div 50$$
$$7 = R$$

Replace the cost with the value given in the question (£450) and solve the equation.

So Si has 7 parts replaced on his car.

Practice Question

1) Hiring a canoe costs £8 per hour plus a £10 deposit. Lily paid £34.
How long did she hire the canoe for?

Number Patterns and Sequences

Sequences are just patterns of numbers or shapes that follow a rule.
You need to be able to spot what the rule is.

Finding **Number Patterns**

The trick to <u>finding the rule</u> for number patterns is to <u>write down</u> what you have to do
to get from one number to the next in the <u>gaps</u> between the numbers.
There are <u>2 main types</u> to look out for:

1) Arithmetic sequences — Add or subtract the same number each time

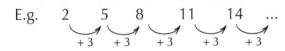

E.g.   2   5   8   11   14   ...   30   24   18   12   ...

        +3   +3   +3   +3   +3   −6   −6   −6   −6

The RULE: 'Add 3 to the <u>previous term</u>'   'Subtract 6 from the <u>previous term</u>'

2) Geometric sequences — Multiply or divide by the same number each time

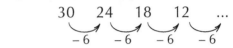

E.g.   2   6   18   54   ...   40 000   4000   400   40   ...

          ×3   ×3   ×3   ×3   ÷10   ÷10   ÷10   ÷10

The RULE: 'Multiply the <u>previous term</u> by 3'   'Divide the <u>previous term</u> by 10'

You might get number patterns that follow a <u>different</u> rule — for example, you might have
to add or subtract a <u>changing number</u> each time, or add together the <u>two previous terms</u>.
You just need to <u>describe</u> the pattern and use your <u>rule</u> to find the next terms.

Shape Patterns

If you have a pattern of <u>shapes</u>, you need to be able to <u>continue</u> the pattern. You might also
have to find the <u>rule</u> for the pattern to work out <u>how many</u> shapes there'll be in a later pattern.

--- Example ---

Here are some patterns made of squares.

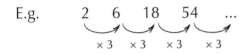

a) Draw the next pattern in the sequence.
b) Work out how many squares there will be in the 6th pattern.

a) Just continue the pattern — add an extra
    square to each of the three legs.

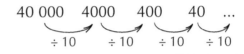

b) Set up a <u>table</u> to find the rule:

Pattern number	1	2	3	4	5	6
Number of squares	1	4	7	10	13	16

The rule is '**add 3 to the previous term**'. So just keep on <u>adding 3</u>
to extend the table until you get to the 6th term — which is **16**.

Practice Question

Remember, you always need to work out how to get from one term to the next — that's the rule.

1) Find the rule and write down the next term in the sequence that starts 38, 32, 26, 20

Number Patterns and Sequences

Finding the *Anything-th* Term

You need to be able to find any term in a sequence without having to count all the way. For sequences with a <u>common difference</u> — where you <u>add</u> or <u>subtract</u> the <u>same number</u> each time, you can find the <u>term</u> from the <u>term number</u> like this.

Example

Find the 40th term of the sequence that starts 5, 9, 13, 17, ...

term number:	1	2	3	4
term:	5	9	13	17

+ 4   + 4   + 4

1) Find the rule for getting the term from the term number by first finding the <u>difference</u> between each term. Here, it's <u>4</u>.

term number × 4:	4	8	12	16
	+ 1	+ 1	+ 1	+ 1
term:	5	9	13	17

2) <u>Multiply</u> the <u>term number</u> by the <u>difference</u>.
3) Work out how to get from the <u>term number × 4</u> to the <u>corresponding term</u>.

The rule is multiply the term number by 4 and add 1

So the 40th term is 40 × 4 + 1 = 161

4) Write down the rule and <u>check</u> it. (For term 3: 3 × 4 + 1 = 13 ✓)
5) Use the rule to find the <u>40th term</u>.

The *nth* Term

The *n*th term is an <u>expression</u> for the term with term number <u>*n*</u>. Here's how to find one.

Example

 Find an expression for the *n*th term of the sequence that starts 2, 8, 14, 20, ...

n:	1	2	3	4
term:	2	8	14	20

+ 6   + 6   + 6

1) Find the <u>common difference</u>. It's <u>6</u>, so this tells you '<u>6*n*</u>' is in the formula.

6*n*:	6	12	18	24
	− 4	− 4	− 4	− 4
term:	2	8	14	20

2) List the values of <u>6*n*</u>.
3) Work out what you have to <u>add</u> or <u>subtract</u> to get from 6*n* to the term. So it's <u>−4</u>

So the expression for the *n*th term is 6*n* − 4

4) Put '<u>6*n*</u>' and '<u>−4</u>' together.

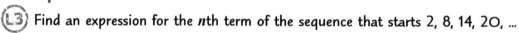
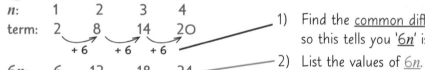

Check your formula by putting the first few values of *n* back in:
$n = 1$ gives $6n - 4 = 6 - 4 = 2$ ✓
$n = 2$ gives $6n - 4 = 12 - 4 = 8$ ✓

Using the *nth* Term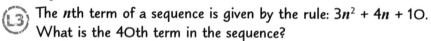

Sometimes you'll be given the <u>rule</u> for a sequence and you have to work out what the 10th, 50th or <u>anything-th</u> term is. This method works for <u>any</u> type of sequence.

Example

The *n*th term of a sequence is given by the rule: $3n^2 + 4n + 10$.
What is the 40th term in the sequence?

1) Write out the expression.

2) Replace *n* with 40.

3) Calculate using BODMAS. First do the <u>square</u>...

4) ...then the <u>multiplications</u> and finally the <u>addition</u>.

$3n^2 + 4n + 10$
$= 3 \times 40^2 + 4 \times 40 + 10$
$= 3 \times 1600 + 4 \times 40 + 10$
$= 4800 + 160 + 10 = 4970$

Practice Questions

1) A sequence starts 15, 23, 31, ...   a) Find the rule to give any term.   b) Find the 28th term.

(L3) 2) Write down a formula for the *n*th term of the sequence in question 1

Inequalities

Inequalities aren't too bad — you just have to find the values which make the statement true.

Using the **Inequality Symbols**

> $>$ means 'Greater than' $\geq$ means 'Greater than or equal to'
>
> $<$ means 'Less than' $\leq$ means 'Less than or equal to'

The one at the BIG end is BIGGEST so $x > 4$ and $4 < x$ both say: 'x is greater than 4'

— **Example** —

Write down all possible values of x in these inequalities.

a) x is a positive integer such that $x \leq 3$

b) x is a negative integer such that $-5 < x$.

Integers are just whole numbers (don't get caught out — 0 is neither positive or negative).

x is a <u>positive</u> integer that is <u>less than or equal to</u> 3   1, 2, 3

x is a <u>negative</u> integer that is <u>greater than</u> −5   −4, −3, −2, −1

Sometimes an inequality will contain <u>more than one</u> symbol. Here's how you tackle those ones.

— **Example** —

If x is an integer such that $-2 < x \leq 4$, write down all possible values of x.

1) Work out what <u>each bit</u> of the inequality is telling you:

$-2 < x$ means that x is greater than −2

$x \leq 4$ means that x is less than or equal to 4

2) Now just write down <u>all the values</u> that x can take: −1, 0, 1, 2, 3, 4

Solving Inequalities

You might have to do a bit of <u>rearranging</u> before you get an inequality with x on its own. This is called <u>solving</u>. You can treat inequalities <u>almost the same</u> as equations — just pretend that the '>' is a '='. The only thing that's different is <u>dividing</u> by a <u>negative</u> number — you have to <u>reverse</u> the <u>inequality sign</u>. It's usually easier to add x's to both sides to get rid of any <u>negative x's</u>.

— **Example** —

Solve $6 - x > 2x + 3$

$$6 - x > 2x + 3$$

$(+ x)$ $6 - x + x > 2x + 3 + x$

The opposite of $-x$ is $+x$, so add x to both sides.

$$6 > 3x + 3$$

$(- 3)$ $6 - 3 > 3x + 3 - 3$

The opposite of $+3$ is -3, so subtract 3 from both sides.

$$3 > 3x$$

$(\div 3)$ $3 \div 3 > 3x \div 3$

The opposite of $\times 3$ is $\div 3$, so divide both sides by 3

$$1 > x$$

Practice Questions

1) Write down all positive integers that satisfy the inequality $5 > x$.

2) Solve: a) $4x - 3 > 5$ b) $3x - 20 \geq 15 - 2x$

Inequalities

Solving **Two Inequalities** Together

You could be given <u>two inequalities</u> and asked to solve them both <u>together</u>. All you have to do here is to <u>solve</u> each one, then write down what they tell you <u>together</u>.

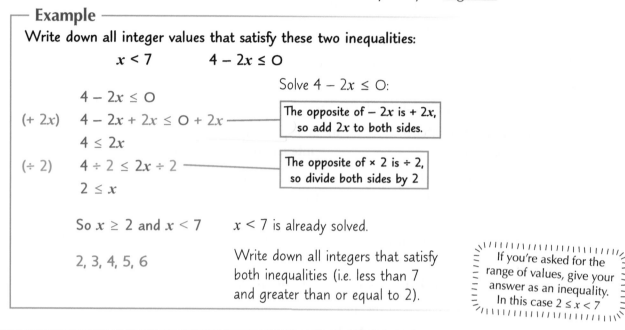

— **Example** —

Write down all integer values that satisfy these two inequalities:

$$x < 7 \qquad 4 - 2x \leq 0$$

Solve $4 - 2x \leq 0$:

	$4 - 2x \leq 0$
(+ 2x)	$4 - 2x + 2x \leq 0 + 2x$
	$4 \leq 2x$
(÷ 2)	$4 \div 2 \leq 2x \div 2$
	$2 \leq x$

The opposite of $-2x$ is $+2x$, so add $2x$ to both sides.

The opposite of $\times 2$ is $\div 2$, so divide both sides by 2

So $x \geq 2$ and $x < 7$ $x < 7$ is already solved.

2, 3, 4, 5, 6   Write down all integers that satisfy both inequalities (i.e. less than 7 and greater than or equal to 2).

If you're asked for the range of values, give your answer as an inequality. In this case $2 \leq x < 7$

You Can Show Inequalities on **Number Lines**

Drawing inequalities on a <u>number line</u> is dead easy — all you have to remember is that you use an <u>open circle</u> (O) for > or < and a <u>coloured-in circle</u> (●) for ≥ or ≤.

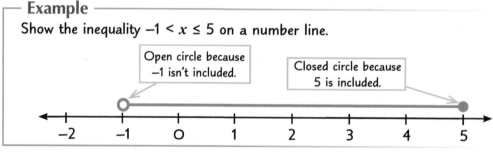

— **Example** —

Show the inequality $-1 < x \leq 5$ on a number line.

Open circle because −1 isn't included.

Closed circle because 5 is included.

An <u>arrow</u> simply means that the line keeps going on <u>forever</u>.

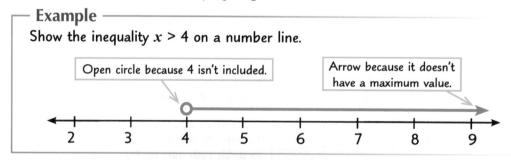

— **Example** —

Show the inequality $x > 4$ on a number line.

Open circle because 4 isn't included.

Arrow because it doesn't have a maximum value.

Practice Question

Be careful with < and > — the number next to them is not included. Have a go at these:

1) a) Write down all integer values that satisfy $x + 3 < 12$ and $\frac{x}{2} + 3 \geq 4$

    b) Show the range of values that satisfy both inequalities in part a) on a number line.

Simultaneous Equations

Simultaneous equations are two equations that you solve at the same time. The method of solving them is a little bit tricky. That's why there's a lovely six-step approach for you to learn. Follow it exactly and you'll be on to a winner.

Six Steps for **Simultaneous Equations**

Example

Solve the simultaneous equations $x = 3y - 10$ and $-2 + 2y = 3x$.

1) <u>Rearrange both equations</u> into the form $\underline{ax + by = c}$, and label the two equations ① and ②.

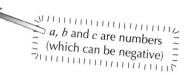

a, b and c are numbers (which can be negative)

$x - 3y = -10$ — ①

$-3x + 2y = 2$ — ②

2) <u>Match up the numbers in front</u> (the 'coefficients') of either the x's or y's in both equations. You may need to multiply one or both equations by a suitable number. Relabel them ③ and ④.

① × 3: $3x - 9y = -30$ — ③

$-3x + 2y = 2$ — ④

Multiply every term in ① by 3 to get a 3 in front of the x.

3) <u>Add or subtract the two equations</u> to eliminate terms with the same number in front of x or y.

③ + ④ $0x - 7y = -28$

If the coefficients have <u>the same sign</u> (both +ve or both −ve) then <u>subtract</u>. If the coefficients have <u>opposite signs</u> (one +ve and one −ve) then <u>add</u>.

4) <u>Solve</u> the resulting equation.

$-7y = -28$

(÷ −7) $-7y \div -7 = -28 \div -7$

$\underline{y = 4}$

5) <u>Substitute</u> the value you've found back into equation ① and <u>solve</u> it to find the other value.

Sub $y = 4$ into ①: $x - (3 \times 4) = -10$

$x - 12 = -10$

(+ 12) $x - 12 + 12 = -10 + 12$

$\underline{x = 2}$

6) <u>Substitute both</u> these values into equation ② to make sure it works. If it doesn't then you've done something wrong and you'll have to do it all again.

Sub x and y into ②: $(-3 \times 2) + (2 \times 4) = -6 + 8 = 2$, which is right, so it's worked.

So the solutions are: $x = 2$, $y = 4$

Practice Questions

1) Find x and y when $x + 4y = 14$ and $6y - x = 6$

2) At Di's Discs, CDs cost £x and DVDs cost £y. Jack bought 3 CDs and 2 DVDs and spent £26. Jill bought 4 CDs and 1 DVD and spent £23.

   a) Write two equations in terms of x and y to show how much Jack and Jill each spent.

   b) Solve these two equations simultaneously to find the cost of CDs and DVDs.

Summary Questions

There was a lot of <u>nasty algebra</u> in that section — let's see how much you remember.

- Try these questions and <u>tick off each one</u> when you <u>get it right</u>.
- When you've done <u>all the questions</u> for a topic and are <u>completely happy</u> with it, tick off the topic

(L1) <u>Algebra (p28-31)</u> ☐

1) Simplify: a) $a + a + a + a$ b) $3b + 8b - 2b$ c) $d + 3e + 5d - 2e$ ☑

2) Simplify: a) $g \times g \times g$ b) $(ab)^2$ c) $(2mn)^3$ d) $\dfrac{6g}{24}$ ☑

3) Expand: a) $3(v + 8)$ b) $-7(2w + 5)$ ☐

4) Expand and simplify $4(3y - 4) - 2$ ☑

5) Factorise: a) $3x + 9$ b) $7x + 21y$ ☑

(L3) 6) Factorise fully: a) $5g^2 - 2g$ b) $6h + 12h^2$ c) $9j^2k + 15jk^2$ ☐

(L1) <u>Solving Equations (p32-34)</u> ☐

7) Solve: a) $x + 12 = 19$ b) $2x = 14$ c) $3x + 5 = 14$ d) $\dfrac{x}{3} = 2$ ☑

(L2) 8) Solve: a) $10 = 5x - 4$ b) $8(x - 2) = 4x$ ☑

(L3) 9) Solve: a) $\dfrac{1}{4}(3x - 2) = 2x - 3$ b) $\dfrac{x^2}{2} = 18$ c) $x(x + 8) = 2(4x + 32)$ ☐

(L3) 10) Use trial and improvement to find the positive solution to the equation $4x^2 - 6x - 8 = 100$ ☐

(L3) 11) A solution to the equation $2y(y - 2) = 100$ lies between 8 and 9
Use trial and improvement to find this solution to 1 decimal place. ☐

(L1) <u>Formulas and Expressions (p35-36)</u> ☐

12) Work out the value of $4m + 7n$ when $m = -2$ and $n = 3$ ☑

(L3) 13) Find q if $p = 2q - 3$ and $p = 15$ ☑

14) Bo goes shopping and buys s steaks (at £7 each) and f fish (at £4 each).
He spends £P in total. Write a formula for P in terms of s and f. ☑

(L1) <u>Number Patterns and Sequences (p37-38)</u> ☐

15) For each of the following sequences, find the next term and write down the rule you used.
a) 2, 8, 14, 20, ... b) 3, 9, 27, 81, ... c) 2, 3, 5, 8, 13, ... ☐

(L2) 16) Write a rule to find any term of the sequence that starts 3, 9, 15, ... from the term number. ☐

(L3) 17) Find an expression for the nth term of the sequence that starts 5, 7, 9, 11, ... ☐

(L3) 18) Find the 6th term of the sequence with nth term $9n^2 + 1$ ☐

(L3) <u>Inequalities (p39-40)</u> ☐

19) Find all the possible positive integer values of x: a) $x < 7$ b) $7 < x \leq 11$ ☑

20) Write down all the integer values of x which satisfy the inequality $-3 \leq x < 6$ ☐

21) Write down all the integer values that satisfy these two inequalities: $y - 4 > 5,\ 10 \geq y$ ☑

22) Solve: a) $x - 4 > 2x + 3$ b) $9 - 4x < 2x - 3$ ☑

23) Show the inequality $-4 < x < 4$ on a number line. ☐

(L3) <u>Simultaneous Equations (p41)</u> ☐

24) Solve these equations simultaneously: $4x - y = 3$ and $3x + 2y = 16$ ☐

Section 2 — Algebra

X and Y Coordinates

What could be more fun than points in one quadrant? Points in four quadrants, that's what...

The Four **Quadrants**

A graph has <u>four different quadrants</u> (regions).

The top-right region is the easiest because
<u>ALL THE COORDINATES IN IT ARE POSITIVE.</u>

You have to be careful in the <u>other regions</u> though,
because the x- and y- coordinates could be <u>negative</u>,
and that makes life much more difficult.

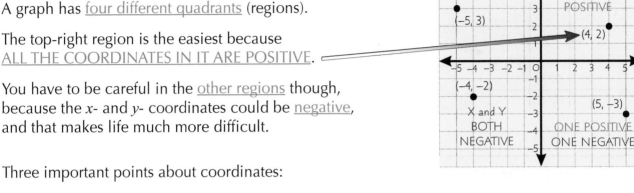

Three important points about coordinates:

(x, y)

1) The coordinates are always in <u>ALPHABETICAL ORDER, x then y</u>.

2) x is always the flat axis going <u>ACROSS</u> the page.
   In other words 'x is a...cross'. Get it — x is a '$\times$'.

3) Remember it's always <u>IN THE HOUSE</u> ($\rightarrow$) and then <u>UP THE STAIRS</u> ($\uparrow$)
   so it's <u>ALONG first</u> and <u>then UP</u>, i.e. x-coordinate first, and then y-coordinate.

The **Midpoint** of a Line

The '<u>MIDPOINT OF A LINE SEGMENT</u>' is the <u>POINT THAT'S BANG IN THE MIDDLE</u> of the line.

Finding the <u>coordinates</u> of a midpoint is
pretty easy. Just learn these <u>three steps</u>...

1) Find the <u>average</u> of the <u>x-coordinates</u>.
2) Find the <u>average</u> of the <u>y-coordinates</u>.
3) Put them in <u>brackets</u>.

Example

 R and S have coordinates (1, 1) and (5, 6).
Find the <u>midpoint</u> of the line RS.

Average of x-coordinates $= \dfrac{1+5}{2} = 3$

Average of y-coordinates $= \dfrac{1+6}{2} = 3.5$

Coordinates of midpoint = (3, 3.5)

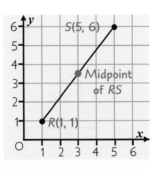

Practice Questions

1) Draw a coordinate grid for x and y from –8 to 8 and plot the points $A(2, -4)$ and $B(-7, 6)$.

2) M and N have coordinates (–4, 2) and (2, –1). Find the midpoint of the line MN.

Straight Line Graphs

Over the next few pages you'll get to see all sorts of straight lines. You're in for a treat.

Vertical and *Horizontal* Lines: 'x = a' and 'y = a'

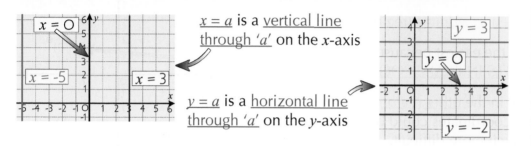

$x = a$ is a <u>vertical line</u> <u>through 'a' on the x-axis</u>

$y = a$ is a <u>horizontal line</u> <u>through 'a' on the y-axis</u>

Remember — all the points on $x = 3$ have an <u>x-coordinate of 3</u>, and all the points on $y = 3$ have a <u>y-coordinate of 3</u>

The *Main Diagonals*: 'y = x' and 'y = −x'

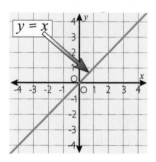

'<u>$y = x$</u>' is the <u>main</u> <u>diagonal</u> that goes <u>UPHILL</u> from left to right.

The x- and y-coordinates of each point are <u>the same</u>, e.g. (4, 4).

'<u>$y = −x$</u>' is the <u>main</u> <u>diagonal</u> that goes <u>DOWNHILL</u> from left to right.

The x- and y-coordinates of each point are <u>negatives</u> <u>of each other</u>, e.g. (−4, 4).

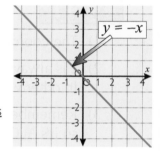

Other Lines Through the *Origin*: 'y = ax' and 'y = −ax'

$y = ax$ and $y = −ax$ are the equations for A SLOPING LINE THROUGH THE ORIGIN.

The value of '<u>a</u>' (known as the <u>gradient</u>) tells you the steepness of the line. The bigger 'a' is, the steeper the slope. A <u>MINUS SIGN</u> tells you it slopes <u>DOWNHILL</u>.

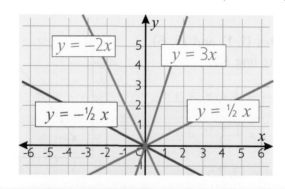

You can <u>rearrange</u> a straight line equation to look like $y = mx + c$, where m is the <u>gradient</u> and c is where the line <u>crosses</u> the y-axis.

Practice Questions

1) Point P has coordinates (2, 4).   a) Which vertical line goes through point P?

       b) Which horizontal line goes through point P?

2) Describe what the line $y = −4x$ looks like.

Plotting Straight Line Graphs

It's likely you'll have to draw a straight line graph in the exam, so learn this method —
it'll lead you to the correct answer every time:

1) Choose <u>3 values of x</u> and <u>draw up a table</u>,

2) <u>Work out the corresponding y-values</u>,

3) <u>Plot the coordinates</u>, and <u>draw the line</u>.

You might get lucky and be given a table to complete in the exam. Don't worry if it contains more than 3 values — just complete it all in the same way.

Doing the 'Table of Values'

Example

Draw the graph of $y = 2x + 1$ for values of x from −3 to 2

1) <u>Choose 3 easy x-values for your table</u>:
Use x-values from the range you're given.
The question might give you the x-values.

x	−1	0	1
y			

2) <u>Find the y-values</u> by putting
each x-value into the equation:

x	−1	0	1
y	−1	1	3

When $x = -1$,
$y = 2x + 1$
$= (2 \times -1) + 1 = -1$

When $x = 1$,
$y = 2x + 1$
$= (2 \times 1) + 1 = 3$

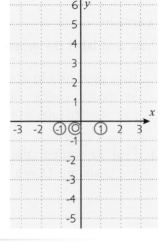

Plotting the Points and Drawing the Graph

Example

...continued from above.

3) <u>Plot each pair</u> of x- and y-values from your table.

The table gives the coordinates:
(−1, −1), (0, 1) and (1, 3).

4) Now draw a <u>straight line</u> through your points
and label it with the <u>equation</u> of the line.
Remember to extend the line through
all the x-values given in the question.

If one point looks a bit wacky, check 2 things:
– the <u>y-value</u> you worked out in the table
– that you've <u>plotted</u> it properly.

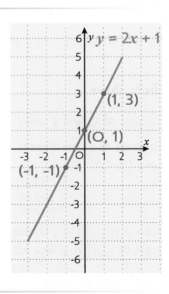

Practice Question

If you have to plot an equation like $3x + y = 6$, you'll have to do a bit of rearranging before you
can find the y-values, or you could use the '$x = 0$, $y = 0$' method (see the next page).

1) a) Plot a table of values for $y + 2x = 4$

b) Draw the graph of $y + 2x = 4$ for values of x from −2 to 2

Section 3 — Graphs

Plotting Straight Line Graphs

Here's another method you need to know for drawing straight line graphs.
Again, you find points on the line using the equation, but just two points this time.

Using the 'x = 0, y = 0' Method

1) Put $x = 0$ into the equation and <u>find y</u> — this is where it <u>crosses the y-axis</u>.
2) Put $y = 0$ into the equation and <u>find x</u> — this is where it <u>crosses the x-axis</u>.
3) <u>Plot these two points</u> and <u>draw a straight line</u> through them.

You can set x and y equal to other numbers, but using zero usually makes the maths easier.

Example

Draw and label the graph of $3x + y = 6$ on the grid below.

1) It's a good idea to draw up a <u>table of values</u> for the <u>two points</u>. Fill in $x = 0$ for the first pair of coordinates and $y = 0$ for the second.

x	0	
y		0

2) <u>Find the missing values</u> by putting $x = 0$ and $y = 0$ into the equation.

x	0	2
y	6	0

$x = 0$ gives:
$(3 \times 0) + y = 6$
$0 + y = 6$,
so $y = 6$

$y = 0$ gives:
$3x + 0 = 6$
$3x = 6$,
so $x = 2$

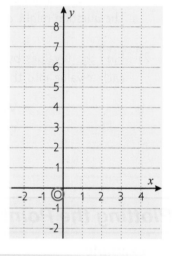

Once you've got your <u>two points</u>, just plot them as usual.

Example

...continued from above.

3) <u>Plot both pairs</u> of x- and y-values from your table.

The table gives the coordinates
$(0, 6)$ and $(2, 0)$.

One point should lie on the x-axis and the other should lie on the y-axis.

4) Finally draw a <u>straight line</u> through your points.
Don't forget to <u>label</u> your line with its equation.

Make sure you double check you've plotted your points accurately — with just two points it's harder to spot mistakes.

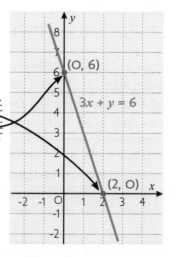

Practice Question

1) a) For the equation $y - 2x = 2$, find y when $x = 0$ and find x when $y = 0$
   b) Use your answers to part a) to draw the graph of $y - 2x = 2$ for x from -3 to 3

Reading Off Graphs

Here's a nice little page for you on reading graphs. At last, the graphs make themselves useful.

Getting Answers from a Graph

You can read values from a
graph using this method:

1) <u>Draw a straight line</u> to the graph from <u>one axis</u>.
2) Then <u>draw a straight line</u> down or across to <u>the other axis</u>.

> **Example**
>
> **Look at this graph of y against x.**
>
> **a) Find the value of x when <u>$y = 5$</u>**
>
> Draw a line <u>across from the y-axis</u> to the
> graph at $y = 5$ and then <u>down to the x-axis</u>.
>
> $x = 5$
>
> **b) Find the value of y when <u>$x = 3$</u>**
>
> Draw a line <u>up from the x-axis</u> to the graph
> at $x = 3$ and then <u>across to the y-axis</u>.
>
> $y \approx 3.3$
>
> $\approx$ means 'is
> approximately
> equal to'.
>
> The answer might not be
> exactly on a grid line. Here
> it's between the 3.2 line and
> the 3.4 line, so it's about 3.3

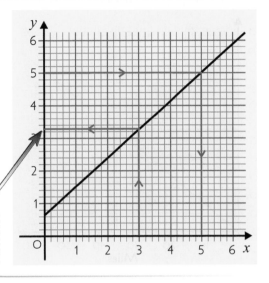

Reading Off *Travel* Graphs

A <u>travel graph</u> is a graph made up of <u>different straight lines</u>,
showing the <u>stages</u> in a journey something makes.

1) A <u>TRAVEL GRAPH</u> is always <u>DISTANCE</u> (↑) against <u>TIME</u> (→).
2) <u>FLAT SECTIONS</u> are where it's <u>STOPPED</u>.
3) The <u>STEEPER</u> the graph the <u>FASTER</u> it's going.
4) The graph <u>GOING UP</u> means it's travelling <u>AWAY</u>.
5) The graph <u>COMING DOWN</u> means it's <u>COMING BACK AGAIN</u>.

> **Example**
>
> **This travel graph shows a morning car journey.**
>
> **a) How far away from home was the car the 2nd time it stopped?**
>
> The car is <u>stopped</u> during the <u>flat parts</u> of the graph.
> <u>Read off</u> the <u>distance</u> at the start of the <u>2nd</u> flat section.   **50 km**
>
> **b) When was the car travelling fastest?**
>
> The car was <u>travelling fastest</u> at the <u>steepest</u> part of the graph.
>
> **9 am to 9:30 am**

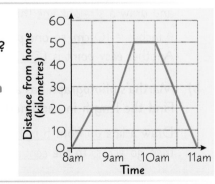

Practice Question

1) Use the graph at the top of the page to find the value of y when $x = 2$

Conversion Graphs

Yay, just what you wanted to see — more graphs...

Conversion Graphs

These are really easy if you remember the <u>method</u> for <u>reading graphs</u> on page 47.
Conversion graphs are used to <u>convert</u> between things like £ and dollars or mph and km/h, etc.

> ### Example
>
> **The conversion graph below can be used to convert between miles and kilometres.**
>
>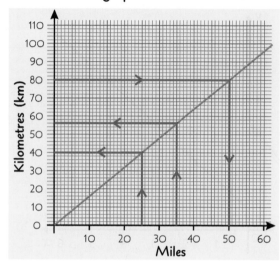
>
> **a)** **Convert 25 miles into kilometres.**
> Draw a line <u>up</u> from 25 on the miles axis 'til
> it <u>hits the line</u>, then go <u>across</u> to the km axis.
> 40 km
>
> **b)** **Convert 80 kilometres into miles.**
> Draw a line <u>across</u> from 80 on the km axis 'til
> it <u>hits the line</u>, then go <u>down</u> to the miles axis.
> 50 miles
>
> **c)** **Find how many kilometres are equal to 35 miles.**
> The answer is 3 grid lines <u>above</u> 50 km, so you
> need to <u>work out</u> what the <u>scale</u> of the graph shows.
> Each <u>grid line</u> on the <u>y-axis</u> represents <u>2 km</u>.
> 50 + (3 × 2) = 56 km

Drawing Your Own Conversion Graph (L2)

Exam questions sometimes ask you to <u>draw</u> the <u>conversion line</u> first — harsh, but true. You'll be
given the information you need — use it to find at least <u>two points</u> to draw your straight line with.

> ### Example
>
> (L2) Martha has an old photograph. She knows its length in inches,
> but wants to convert the length into centimetres.
>
> **a)** **Using 4 inches = 10 cm, draw a line on the graph
> to convert lengths up to 6 inches into centimetres.**
>
> Work out the coordinates of <u>two points</u> on the line
> and draw a <u>straight line</u> through them.
>
> 4 inches = 10 cm, so one point is <u>(4, 10)</u>.
> Another easy point is <u>(0, 0)</u>.
>
> **b)** **Martha's photograph has a length of 5 inches.
> Find the length in centimetres.**
>
> Draw a line <u>up</u> from <u>5 inches</u> to the line,
> then go <u>across</u> to the <u>centimetres</u> axis.   12.5 cm
>
>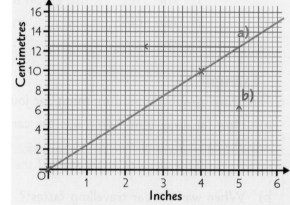
>
> Make sure you show your working lines clearly.

Practice Question

1) Use the conversion graph at the bottom of the page to convert 5 cm into inches.

Solving Simultaneous Equations

Solving simultaneous equations is just a mathsy way of saying "solving two equations at the same time". You can solve them using algebra (see p.41), or by drawing their graphs.

Solving **Simultaneous Equations** Using Graphs

To solve <u>two equations simultaneously</u>, you need to find values of <u>x and y</u> that make <u>both equations true</u>. Luckily there's an easy way to find them.

The <u>solution</u> of two simultaneous equations is simply the x- and y-values <u>where their graphs cross</u>.

Here's the general <u>method</u> to follow:

1) <u>Draw</u> the two graphs.

2) Find the <u>x- and y-values</u> where they <u>cross</u>.

3) Put the values back into <u>both equations</u> to check they work.

The point where the lines cross is called the point of intersection.

Example

Use this graph to solve the equations
$y = 3x + 1$ and $y = 5 - x$ simultaneously.

The graphs are drawn for you so jump straight to step 2

Find the <u>x-value</u> and the <u>y-value</u> $x = 1$
where the <u>two lines cross</u>. $y = 4$
<u>Check</u> the values — put the <u>x-value</u>
into each equation and check it $y = (3 \times 1) + 1 = 4$ ✓
gives you the correct <u>y-value</u>. $y = 5 - 1 = 4$ ✓

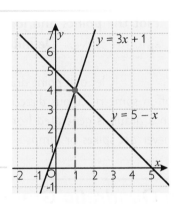

Exam questions might take you through the method in <u>stages</u>.

Example

Using the grid opposite:

a) Draw the graph of $x - y = -1$
   by completing this table of values.

x	O	−1
y	1	O

   Find the <u>missing values</u> by putting
   $x = O$ and $y = O$ into the equation.
   Then <u>plot</u> the points and <u>draw the line</u>.

b) Draw the graph of $4x + y = 6$
   by completing this table of values.

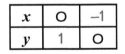

x	O	1
y	6	2

   Find the <u>missing values</u> by putting
   $x = O$ and $y = 2$ into the equation.
   Then <u>plot</u> the points and <u>draw the line</u>.

This y-value makes the numbers easy.

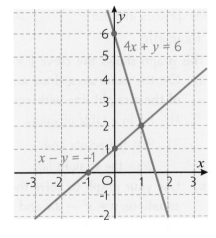

c) Write down the solution to the equations $x - y = -1$ and $4x + y = 6$

   Read off the <u>x- and y-values</u> where the $x = 1$ $y = 2$
   <u>lines cross</u> and <u>check</u> they work. $1 - 2 = -1$ ✓ $(4 \times 1) + 2 = 6$ ✓

Practice Question

1) a) Draw the graphs of $y = 2x - 2$ and $y = 4 - x$ on the same axes.
   b) Solve the simultaneous equations $y = 2x - 2$ and $y = 4 - x$.

Quadratic Graphs

These quadratic graphs have lovely smooth curves — more of a test for your graph-drawing skills.

Drawing a **Quadratic Graph**

Quadratic graphs are of the form
$y = \underline{\text{anything with } x^2}$ (but not higher powers of x).
They all have the same <u>symmetrical</u>
bucket shape, called a <u>parabola</u>.

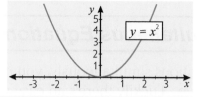

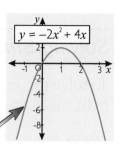

If the x^2 bit has a '−' in front of it
then the bucket is <u>upside down</u>.

Example

Complete the table of values for the equation
$y = x^2 - 1$ and then draw the graph.

x	−3	−2	−1	0	1	2	3
y	8	3	0	−1	0	3	8

1) Work out each <u>y-value</u> by <u>substituting</u> the corresponding <u>x-value</u> into the equation.

$\underline{x = -2}$: $y = (-2)^2 - 1 = 4 - 1 = 3$
$\underline{x = 1}$: $y = (1)^2 - 1 = 1 - 1 = 0$

2) Plot the points and join them with a <u>completely smooth curve</u>. Definitely <u>DON'T</u> use a ruler.

<u>NEVER EVER</u> let one point drag your
line off in some ridiculous direction.
When a graph is generated from an equation,
you never get spikes or lumps — only <u>MISTAKES</u>.

This point is
<u>obviously wrong</u>

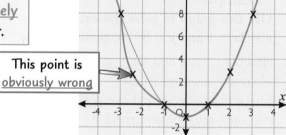

Using **Quadratic Graphs** to Solve **Simultaneous Equations**

A <u>quadratic</u> and a <u>straight line</u> graph can cross at <u>two points</u> (two <u>points of intersection</u>).
These points are the <u>solutions</u> to the <u>simultaneous equations</u> shown on the graph.

Example

This graph shows the curve $y = x^2 - 2x$.

a) On the same axes, draw and label the graph
of the straight line with equation $y = 2x + 5$

1) Fill in a <u>table of values</u>.

2) Plot the points and
draw the <u>straight line</u>.

x	−2	0	2
y	1	5	9

b) Use your graph to solve the simultaneous
equations $y = x^2 - 2x$ and $y = 2x + 5$.

The line crosses the curve at (−1, 3) and (5, 15)
So your solutions are $x = -1$, $y = 3$ and $x = 5$, $y = 15$
<u>Check</u> the values:
$y = (-1)^2 - 2(-1) = 3$ ✓ $y = 2(-1) + 5 = 3$ ✓
$y = 5^2 - 2(5) = 15$ ✓ $y = 2(5) + 5 = 15$ ✓

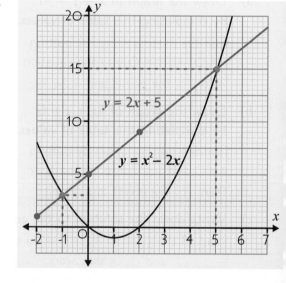

Practice Question

1) a) Draw the graphs of $y = x^2 + 3$ and $y = 2x + 6$ on a set of axes with x from −3 to 3
   b) Write down the solutions to the simultaneous equations $y = x^2 + 3$ and $y = 2x + 6$

Summary Questions

Well, that wraps up <u>Section 3</u> — time to test yourself and find out <u>how much you really know</u>.
- Try these questions and <u>tick off each one</u> when you <u>get it right</u>.
- When you've done <u>all the questions</u> for a topic and are <u>completely happy</u> with it, tick off the topic.

(L1) <u>Coordinates (p43)</u> ☐

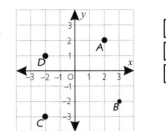

1) Give the coordinates of points A to D in the diagram on the right. ☐
2) Find the midpoint of a line segment with endpoints C and D. ☐
(L2) 3) Find the midpoint of a line segment with endpoints A and B. ☐

(L1) <u>Straight Line Graphs (p44)</u> ☐

4) Give the coordinates of one point on each of these lines: a) $x = 4$ b) $y = 2$ ☐
5) Write down the coordinates of the point where the lines $x = 3$ and $y = 1$ intersect. ☐
6) Write down two equations that give vertical lines. ☐
(L2) 7) Say whether the graphs of these equations go uphill, downhill or neither (from left to right):
 a) $y = -2$ b) $y = -3x$ c) $-y + x = 0$ ☐

(L2) <u>Plotting Straight Line Graphs (p45-46)</u> ☐

8) Draw the graph of $y = -3x + 2$ for the values of x from –2 to 2 ☐
9) For the equation $y + 2x = 10$, find y when $x = 0$ and x when $y = 0$
 Use your answers to draw the graph of $y + 2x = 10$ for values of x from –5 to 5 ☑

(L1) <u>Reading Off Graphs (p47-48)</u> ☐

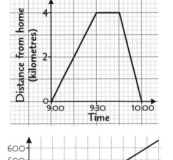

10) Describe the general method for reading values from a graph. ☐
11) The graph on the right shows Bob's bicycle journey
 to the shop and back.
 a) Did he ride faster on his way to the
 shop or on his way home?
 b) How long did he spend in the shop? ☐
12) Use the conversion graph opposite to convert:
 a) 250 pounds to euros b) 600 euros to pounds ☐

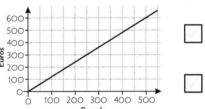

(L2) 13) For a test that is marked out of 20, draw a conversion graph
 to convert marks up to 20 into percentage marks. ☐

(L3) <u>Simultaneous Equations (p49)</u> ☐

14) By drawing the graphs of $y = 2x$ and $y = x + 2$, solve the equations simultaneously. ☐

(L3) <u>Quadratic Graphs (p50)</u> ☐

15) What is the general shape of a quadratic graph? ☑
16) a) Make a table of values for the equation $y = x^2 - 3$ for values of x between –3 and 3
 b) Use your table in part a) to draw the graph of $y = x^2 - 3$
 c) On the same axes draw the graph of $y = -x + 3$
 d) Use your graphs to solve $y = x^2 - 3$ and $y = -x + 3$ simultaneously. ☑

Ratios

Ratios can be a bit nasty, but the examples on the next few pages should cut them down to size.

Reducing **Ratios** to Their **Simplest Form**

To reduce a ratio to a <u>simpler form</u>, divide <u>all the numbers</u> in the ratio by the <u>same thing</u> (a bit like simplifying a fraction). It's in its <u>simplest form</u> when you can't divide anymore to get whole numbers.

> **Example**
>
> Vicky has 25 pork pies and Jonny has 15 pork pies. Write the number of Vicky's pies to Jonny's as a ratio in its simplest form.
>
> 1) First, write the numbers as a <u>ratio</u> — 25:15
>
> 2) <u>Simplify</u> the ratio — both numbers have a <u>factor</u> of 5, so <u>divide them by 5</u>. We can't reduce this any further, so the simplest form of 25:15 is **5:3**
>
> $\div 5 \left(\dfrac{25:15}{5:3} \right) \div 5$

The More **Awkward Cases**:

1) If the ratio contains <u>decimals</u> or <u>fractions</u> — <u>multiply</u> until you reach a whole number, then <u>simplify</u>.

> E.g. To simplify:
>
> $\times 10 \left(\dfrac{1.2:1.5}{12:15} \right) \times 10$
>
> $= \div 3 \left(\dfrac{12:15}{4:5} \right) \div 3$

2) If the ratio has <u>mixed units</u> — convert to the <u>smaller unit</u> before simplifying.

> E.g. To simplify:
>
> 18 mm : 3.6 cm
>
> = 18 mm : 36 mm
>
> $= \div 18 \searrow 1:2 \swarrow \div 18$

If the units are the same, you can remove them.

3) To get to the form <u>1:n</u> or <u>n:1</u> — just <u>divide</u>. <u>Decimals</u> are okay in this case.

> **Example**
>
> Reduce 4:30 to the form 1:*n*.
>
> Divide both sides by 4:　$\div 4 \left(\dfrac{4:30}{1:7.5} \right) \div 4$
>
> *This form is often the most useful, since it shows the ratio very clearly.*

> **Example**
>
> Write the ratio 1.2 kg:200 g in the form *n*:1.
>
> Convert 1.2 kg to 1200 g
> Divide both sides by 200:
>
> $\div 200 \left(\dfrac{1200:200}{6:1} \right) \div 200$

Practice Question

There are lots of different examples on this page, but the method for simplifying them is the same.
1) Simplify the following ratios:　a) 7:63　　b) 2.2:5.5　　c) 8 cm:48 mm

Ratios

Ratios are so exciting (and important) that I decided they needed another page...

Scaling Up **Ratios**

If you know the ratio between parts and the actual size of one part,
you can scale the ratio up to find the other parts.

— Example —

Purple paint is made from red paint and blue paint in the ratio 5:3

a) If 20 pots of red paint are used, how much blue paint is needed?

You need to multiply by 4 to go from 5 to 20 on
the left-hand side (LHS) — so do that to both sides:

So **12 pots** of blue paint are needed.

red paint:blue paint

$= \times 4 \big(\ 5:3 \ \big) \times 4$

$= \quad 20:12$

b) If 20 pots of red paint are used, how many pots of paint are used in total?

Add the number of red and blue pots together.

20 + 12 = **32 pots**

Ratios with 3 parts follow exactly the same rules:

— Example —

(L2) Brenda has a tray of cupcakes, scones and biscuits in the ratio 2:4:6
If she has 18 biscuits on the tray, how many cupcakes, scones and biscuits does she have in total?

1) Multiply each number in the ratio by 3 to go
from 6 to 18 on the right hand side (RHS).

cupcakes:scones:biscuits

$= \times 3 \big(2 \ : \ 4 \ : \ 6 \big) \times 3$

$= \quad 6 \ : \ 12 \ : \ 18$

2) Add together the numbers of
cupcakes, scones and biscuits.

6 + 12 + 18 = **36 cupcakes, scones and biscuits**

Writing a **Fraction** as a **Ratio**

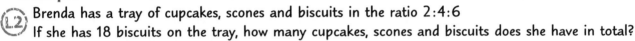

You can rewrite fractions as ratios instead.

— Example —

Micaela owns a collection of 24 hats. $\frac{5}{8}$ of the hats are red and the rest are blue.
What is the ratio of red hats to blue hats?

1) In every 8 hats, 5 hats are red and 8 − 5 = 3 hats are blue.

2) So there are 5 red hats for every 3 blue hats.
Write as a ratio:

Ratio of red to blue hats is **5:3**.

Practice Questions

1) A fruit punch is made from orange juice and apple juice in the ratio 4:7
If 20 litres of orange juice is used, how much apple juice is used?

2) The ratio of first class to economy class passengers on a flight is 2:12.
If there are 108 economy class passengers, how many passengers are there in total?

3) In an office, $\frac{3}{7}$ of the staff are men. What is the ratio of women to men in this office?

Ratios

... and another page. These examples are really important, so make sure you understand them.

Proportional **Division**

In a <u>proportional division</u> question a <u>TOTAL AMOUNT</u> is split into <u>PARTS</u> in a certain ratio. The key word here is <u>PARTS</u> — concentrate on 'parts' and it all becomes quite painless.

Example

If Kim and Chris share £600 in the ratio 4:11, how much does Chris get?

1) <u>ADD UP THE PARTS</u>:
   The ratio 4:11 means there will be a total of 15 <u>parts</u>:   4 + 11 = 15 parts

2) <u>DIVIDE TO FIND ONE "PART"</u>:
   Just divide the <u>total amount</u> by the number of <u>parts</u>:   £600 ÷ 15 = £40   (= 1 part)

3) <u>MULTIPLY TO FIND THE AMOUNTS</u>:
   We want to know <u>Chris's share</u>, which is <u>11 parts</u>:   11 parts = 11 × £40 = £440

Example

Shauna and Roberto have 80 sweets between them. Shauna has 4 times as many sweets as Roberto. How many sweets do they each have?

1) Work out the ratio.   Shauna has 4 sweets to every 1 of Roberto's sweets, so the ratio is 4:1

2) <u>DIVIDE</u> the <u>TOTAL AMOUNT</u> by the number of <u>PARTS</u>.   There are 4 + 1 = 5 parts
        80 ÷ 5 = 16 (= 1 part)

3) Work out each person's share: Roberta has 1 part (16 sweets)
        Shauna has 4 parts (4 × 16 = 64 sweet[s]

Check this by making sure they add up to 80: 16 + 64 = 80.

Part : Whole Ratios

For <u>part : whole</u> ratios the <u>left hand side</u> of the ratio is <u>included in</u> the <u>right hand side</u>.

Example

Mrs Miggins owns some tabby cats and ginger cats.
The ratio of tabby cats to the total number of cats is 3:5.

a) **What fraction of Mrs Miggins' cats are tabby cats?**

   The ratio tells you that for every <u>5 cats</u>, <u>3</u> are tabby cats. $\frac{part}{whole} = \frac{3}{5}$

b) **What is the ratio of tabby cats to ginger cats?**

   3 in every 5 cats are tabby, so 2 in every 5 are ginger.   5 − 3 = 2
   For every <u>3 tabby cats</u>, there are <u>2 ginger cats</u>.   tabby : ginger = 3 : 2

   If you're given a part : part ratio you'll need to add up the total number of parts first.

c) **Mrs Miggins has 35 cats in total. How many ginger cats does she have?**

   1) Find the <u>total</u> number of parts: 5 parts
   2) Divide the <u>total</u> by the number of <u>parts</u>:   35 ÷ 5 parts = 7 (= 1 part)
   3) Multiply to find the number of ginger cats, which is 2 parts: 2 parts = 2 × 7 = 14

Practice Question

1) Ahmed gets a share of a £500 prize. How much money will
   Ahmed get if the ratio of his share to the total amount is 12 : 25?

Direct Proportion

Direct proportions aren't that bad really. Just learn the golden rule and all will be just fine.

Solving Direct Proportion Questions

Direct proportions tell you how <u>one thing increases</u> as <u>another increases</u> at the same rate.
The <u>ratio</u> between the two things <u>stays the same</u>.

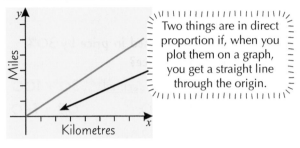

Two things are in direct proportion if, when you plot them on a graph, you get a straight line through the origin.

You can solve all direct proportion questions
if you remember this <u>golden rule</u>:

DIVIDE for ONE, then TIMES for ALL

— **Example** —————————————————————————

3 painters can paint 9 rooms per day.
How many rooms per day could 7 painters paint?

1) Start by <u>dividing by 3</u> to find how many
    rooms <u>1 painter</u> could paint per day. $9 \div 3 = 3$ rooms per day

2) Then <u>multiply by 7</u> to find how many
    rooms <u>7 painters</u> could paint per day. $3 \times 7 = 21$ rooms per day

— **Example** —————————————————————————

(L2) **10 baguettes cost £1.50**

a) **How much will 12 baguettes cost?**
    Start by <u>dividing by 10</u> to find the cost of <u>1 baguette</u>.   £1.50 ÷ 10 = £0.15
    Then <u>multiply by 12</u> to find the cost of <u>12 baguettes</u>.   £0.15 × 12 = £1.80

b) **How many baguettes can be bought with £6?**
    You know the cost of 1 baguette from above.   £0.15
    Just divide £6 by £0.15   6 ÷ 0.15 = 40 baguettes

— **Example** —————————————————————————

(L2) **A recipe for 2 heaps of compost uses 1 kg of eggshells, 2 kg of manure and 3 kg of leaves.**
Work out the recipe for 5 heaps of compost.

1) Work out how much of each waste makes   Eggshells: 1 ÷ 2 = 0.5 kg, Manure: 2 ÷ 2 = 1 kg,
    up 1 compost heap — <u>divide</u> each by <u>2</u>   Leaves: 3 ÷ 2 = 1.5 kg.

2) <u>Multiply</u> each type of waste by <u>5</u>   Eggshells: 0.5 × 5 = 2.5 kg, Manure: 1 × 5 = 5 kg,
                                                          Leaves: 1.5 × 5 = 7.5 kg.

Practice Questions

1) 4 lumberjacks chop 12 trees in a day. How many trees could 13 lumberjacks chop in a day?
2) 15 koalas eat 7.5 kg of eucalyptus per day.
    How much eucalyptus do 18 koalas eat each day?
3) Mary's recipe to make 12 flapjacks requires 252 g oats, 120 g butter and 100 g sugar.
    Find the amounts of oats, butter and sugar needed to make 18 flapjacks.

Percentage Change

Questions about percentage change are a bit trickier than finding basic percentages (see p.22).

Find the **New Amount** After a **% Increase or Decrease**

Turn the percentage into a <u>decimal</u>, then <u>multiply</u>. <u>Add</u> (or <u>subtract</u>) this on to the <u>original value</u>.

— **Examples** —

A £40 dress increased in price by 30%.
What is its new price?

1) Write 30% as a <u>decimal</u>. $30 \div 100 = 0.3$

2) Find 30% <u>of</u> £40: $0.3 \times £40 = £12$

3) It's an increase, so <u>add</u> on
   to the original price: $£40 + £12 = £52$

Decrease 600 ml by 40%.

1) Write 40% as a decimal.
   $$40 \div 100 = 0.4$$

2) Find 40% <u>of</u> 600 ml.
   $$0.4 \times 600 = 240$$

3) It's a decrease, so <u>subtract</u> from the
   original price: $600 - 240 = 360$ ml

Finding the **Percentage Change**

This is the formula for giving a <u>change in value</u> as a <u>percentage</u> — <u>LEARN IT, AND USE IT</u>:

$$\text{Percentage 'Change'} = \frac{\text{'Change'}}{\text{Original}} \times 100$$

Typical questions will ask 'Find the percentage <u>increase</u> / <u>profit</u> / <u>error</u>' or
'Calculate the percentage <u>decrease</u> / <u>loss</u> / <u>discount</u>', etc.

— **Example** —

If a bus fare increases from £2.50 to £3, find the percentage increase.

1) Find the <u>actual increase</u> in price: increase = £3 − £2.50 = £0.50

2) Then use the <u>formula</u>:   percentage increase = $\frac{0.5}{2.5} \times 100 = 20\%$

— **Example** —

The population of a village decreases from 800 to 680 people.
Find the percentage decrease of the village's population.

1) Find the <u>actual decrease</u> in population: decrease = 800 − 680 = 120

2) Then use the <u>formula</u>:   percentage decrease = $\frac{120}{800} \times 100 = 15\%$

Practice Questions

1) A company makes $12 000 profit in January and $30 000 profit in March.
   a) There is a 25% increase in profit from January to February. Find the profit for February.
   b) Calculate the percentage increase from January to March.

2) A painting decreases in value from £8 million to £7.5 million. Find the percentage loss.

Percentage Change

Here's some more on percentage changes — it's a useful real-life skill so make sure you can do it.

Simple *Interest*

Sometimes, a certain percentage of an <u>original amount</u> is added at <u>regular intervals</u>, so the <u>same amount</u> is added <u>every time</u>. <u>Simple interest</u> is where a percentage of an original amount of <u>money</u> is added <u>every year</u>.

--- **Example** ---

Luna starts with £150 in her savings account. Each year, 2% of her original amount is added to her account. How much will she have in her savings account after 6 years?

1)	Write 2% as a <u>decimal</u>.	2 ÷ 100 = 0.02
2)	<u>Multiply</u> 0.02 by £150 to find the money added <u>in 1 year</u>:	0.02 × £150 = £3
3)	Multiply by 6 to get the <u>total amount</u> for <u>6 years</u>:	£3 × 6 = £18
4)	It's an increase, so <u>add</u> on to the original amount:	£150 + £18 = £168

Finding the *Original Value*

When you're given the <u>percentage change</u> and the <u>new value</u>, and you want the <u>original value</u>:

> 1) Write the amount in the question as a <u>percentage of the original value</u>.
> 2) <u>Divide</u> to find <u>1%</u> of the original value and <u>multiply by 100</u> to give the original value.

--- **Example** ---

(L3) John has a collection of vintage vehicles. Over a year, one car decreases in value by 40% to £7200, and one motorbike increases in value by 25% to £8750.

a) Calculate the original value of the car.

1) A <u>decrease</u> of 40% means £7200 represents <u>60% of the original</u> value.

2) Divide by 60 to find <u>1%</u> of the original value.

3) Then multiply by 100.

$$\div 60 \begin{cases} £7200 = 60\% \\ £120 = 1\% \end{cases}$$
$$\times 100 \begin{cases} £12\,000 = 100\% \end{cases}$$

So the original value of the car was £12 000

b) Calculate the original value of the motorbike.

1) An <u>increase</u> of 25% means £8750 represents <u>125% of the original</u> value.

2) Divide by 125 to find <u>1%</u> of the original value.

3) Then multiply by 100.

$$\div 125 \begin{cases} £8750 = 125\% \\ £70 = 1\% \end{cases}$$
$$\times 100 \begin{cases} £7000 = 100\% \end{cases}$$

So the original value of the motorbike was £7000

Practice Questions

1) Arabelle runs a distance of 1800 m. Each week, she increases the distance she runs by 15% of her original distance. What distance does she run after 5 weeks?

(L3) 2) Radiators increase the temperature of a room by 25% to 22.5 °C. What was the temperature of the room before the radiators heated it up?

Metric and Imperial Units

There's nothing too bad on this page — just some facts to learn.

Metric Units

1) <u>Length</u>   mm, cm, m, km
2) <u>Area</u>   mm², cm², m², km², hectares
3) <u>Volume</u>   mm³, cm³, m³, ml, cl, litres
4) <u>Mass</u>   mg, g, kg, tonne
5) <u>Speed</u>   km/h, m/s
6) <u>Temperature</u> °C

'Weight' is often used instead of 'mass' in everyday language.

MEMORISE THESE KEY FACTS:

1 cm = 10 mm	1 ml = 1 cm³
1 m = 100 cm	1 litre = 100 cl
1 km = 1000 m	1 gram = 1000 mg
1 litre = 1000 ml	1 kg = 1000 g
1 litre = 1000 cm³	1 tonne = 1000 kg

Imperial Units

1) <u>Length</u>   inches, feet, yards, miles
2) <u>Area</u>   square inches, square feet, square miles, acres
3) <u>Volume</u>   cubic inches, cubic feet, gallons, pints
4) <u>Mass</u>   ounces, pounds, stones, tons
5) <u>Speed</u>   mph
6) <u>Temperature</u> °F

Don't panic — you don't need to learn these for your exam. But you should recognise the units.

IMPERIAL UNIT CONVERSIONS

1 foot = 12 inches
1 yard = 3 feet
1 gallon = 8 pints
1 stone = 14 pounds (lb)
1 pound = 16 ounces (oz)

Metric-Imperial Conversions

Make sure you learn these <u>approximate conversions</u>.
They'll help you change between <u>metric</u> units and <u>imperial</u> units.

'≈' means 'approximately equal to'.

APPROXIMATE CONVERSIONS

1 inch ≈ 2.5 cm   1 kg ≈ 2.2 pounds (lb)   1 foot ≈ 30 cm
1 litre ≈ 1.75 pints   1 mile ≈ 1.6 km (or 5 miles ≈ 8 km)

3-Step Method for Converting

There are some examples of conversions on the next page.

① Find the <u>conversion factor</u> (always easy).

② Decide whether to <u>multiply</u> or <u>divide</u> by it
(use the <u>conversion factor</u> to decide if the answer should be <u>bigger</u> or <u>smaller</u>).

③ <u>Work out</u> your answer (and <u>check it</u>).

Practice Questions

The conversion factor in the 3-step method is just the number in the conversion, e.g. for
1 m = 100 cm, it's 100. If you don't know whether to multiply or divide by it, you can try both.

1) Convert: a) 3.5 cm to mm   b) 2.8 litres to cm³   c) 4.5 tonnes to kg.
2) Convert: a) 44 lbs to kg   b) 5 feet to cm   c) 20 km to miles.

Section 4 — Ratio, Proportion and Rates of Change

Converting Units

Time to try out the 3-step method for converting (see p.58) — here are lots of fun examples.

Examples

Example

A zoo has a miniature gorilla called Augustus, who is 30 cm tall. How tall is he in m?

1) Find the <u>conversion factor</u>.   1 m = 100 cm, so conversion factor = 100

2) Decide whether to <u>multiply or divide</u> by it. You'd expect more cm than m, so <u>divide</u>

3) Work out the <u>answer</u>.   30 ÷ 100 = 0.3 m | <u>Check</u> your answer — 0.3 is less than 30, so this looks sensible.

Example

Nick lives 18 miles away from his friend Anna. Approximately, how far is this in km?

1) Find the <u>conversion factor</u>.   1 mile ≈ 1.6 km, so conversion factor = 1.6

2) Decide whether to <u>multiply or divide</u> by it.   You'd expect more km than miles, so <u>multiply</u>

3) Work out the <u>answer</u>.   18 × 1.6 = 28.8, so 18 miles ≈ 28.8 km

<u>Check</u> your answer — 28.8 is bigger than 18, so this looks sensible.

Example

Declan owns 5 hectares of land. Use the conversion 1 hectare = 2.47 acres
to work out the area of his land in acres. Give your answer to the nearest whole acre.

1) Find the <u>conversion factor</u> from the question. 1 hectare = 2.47 acres, so conversion factor = 2.47

2) <u>Decide</u> whether to <u>multiply or divide</u> by it.   You'd expect more acres than hectares, so <u>multiply</u>

3) Work out the <u>multiplication</u>.   5 × 2.47 = 12.35 acres

4) Round your <u>answer</u>.   Round 12.35 to the nearest acre = 12 acres

<u>Check</u> your answer — 12 is bigger than 5, so this looks sensible.

Example

Write the following measurements in order of size from smallest to largest:
        180 cm³, 1.75 litres, 185 ml

1) First, write all three measurements in the <u>same unit</u> — I'm going to choose cm³.   1 litre = 1000 cm³ and 1 ml = 1 cm³
So 1.75 litres = 1750 cm³ and 185 ml = 185 cm³

2) Write them out <u>in order</u>.   180 cm³, 185 cm³, 1750 cm³

3) Convert back to the <u>original units</u>.   180 cm³, 185 ml, 1.75 litres

---

Practice Questions

Always check your answer — if you end up with a ridiculously big or ridiculously small number, you probably multiplied when you should have divided or vice versa.

1) Write these measurements in order of size from smallest to largest: 44 mm, 0.5 m, 4.2 cm

2) Convert 26 miles into: a) kilometres   b) metres   c) centimetres

Section 4 — Ratio, Proportion and Rates of Change

More Conversions

Converting areas and volumes from one unit to another is a bit treacherous, because 1 m² does <u>NOT</u> equal 100 cm². Remember this and read on for why.

Converting **Area** and **Volume** Measurements

Be really <u>careful</u> — 1 m = 100 cm <u>DOES NOT</u> mean 1 m² = 100 cm² or 1 m³ = 100 cm³. You won't slip up if you <u>LEARN THESE RULES</u>:

| <u>Area</u>: units come with a <u>2</u>, e.g. mm², cm², m² — <u>use the conversion factor 2 times</u>. | <u>Volume</u>: units come with a <u>3</u>, e.g. mm³, cm³, m³ — <u>use the conversion factor 3 times</u>. |

$$1 \text{ m}^2 = 100 \text{ cm} \times 100 \text{ cm}$$
$$1 \text{ cm}^2 = 10 \text{ mm} \times 10 \text{ mm}$$

$$1 \text{ m}^3 = 100 \text{ cm} \times 100 \text{ cm} \times 100 \text{ cm}$$
$$1 \text{ cm}^3 = 10 \text{ mm} \times 10 \text{ mm} \times 10 \text{ mm}$$

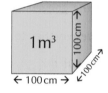

Examples

Convert 5 m² to cm².

To change area measurements from m² to cm² multiply by 100 twice.

5 × 100 × 100 = 50 000 cm²

Convert 80 000 mm³ to cm³.

To change volume measurements from mm³ to cm³ divide by 10 three times.

80 000 ÷ (10 × 10 × 10) = 80 cm³

You should expect your answers to be <u>really big</u> or <u>really small</u> compared to the value you're given — so if they're not, something's gone wrong.

Converting **Speeds**

To convert a speed, you might have to convert both <u>distance</u> and <u>time</u> units. Do it in <u>two stages</u>.

Example

A panther at Birdingbury safari park was recorded running at 54 km/h.
How fast is this in metres per second?

① First convert <u>54 km</u> into <u>m</u>:

1 km = 1000 m, so conversion factor = 1000
You'd expect more m than km, so multiply:
54 × 1000 = 54 000 m/h

② Now convert <u>hours</u> into <u>seconds</u>.

Start with <u>hours</u> into <u>minutes</u>...

There are 60 minutes in an hour, so:
54 000 ÷ 60 = 900 m/minute

... then do <u>minutes</u> into <u>seconds</u>.

There are 60 seconds in a minute, so:
900 ÷ 60 = 15 m/s

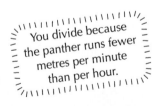

You divide because the panther runs fewer metres per minute than per hour.

Practice Questions

1) Convert: a) 2.4 cm³ into mm³   b) 400 000 cm² into m².

2) The speed limit along a stretch of road is 60 mph. What is this in km/h?

Section 4 — Ratio, Proportion and Rates of Change

Reading Scales and Estimating

There's plenty of useful info to learn on this page — it may even come in handy in real life.

How to **Read** a **Scale**

All scales consist of a <u>line divided into intervals</u>.
To <u>read a point</u> on the scale, you need to
know <u>what each small gap represents</u>:

| Small gap | = | Size of large gap between numbers / Number of small gaps between numbers |

$$\text{Small gap} = \frac{\text{Size of large gap between numbers}}{\text{Number of small gaps between numbers}}$$

1) On the scale to the right there's a
<u>difference of 10</u> between the numbers,
and <u>5 small gaps</u> between them, so
each small gap is worth 10 ÷ 5 = 2 cm.

2) The <u>orange arrow</u> is 3 small gaps after 30 — 3 small
gaps = 3 × 2 = 6, so it's pointing to 30 + 6 = 36 cm.

--- Example ---

Draw 148 km/h on this speedometer.

1) Work out what each
<u>small gap</u> represents.

Large gap = 20
No. of small gaps = 5
Small gap = 20 ÷ 5 = 4 km/h

2) Find the nearest <u>big number before</u> 148. Then work
out how many <u>small gaps</u> you need to <u>add on</u>.

140 + 4 = 144
144 + 4 = 148

So draw the arrow at
140 + 2 small gaps.

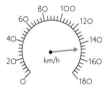

Choosing Units and **Estimating**

Think about what you're being asked to <u>measure</u>. Ask yourself if it's <u>big</u> or
<u>small</u> — then choose the unit that'll give the most sensible answer.

metre	kilometre
centimetre	hectare
millilitre	litre
kilogram	gram

--- Examples ---

Choose the most sensible unit from the box on the right to measure:

a) **The volume of tea in a small mug.**

Find the units used to
measure <u>volume</u>.   Litre and millilitre
<u>Millilitres</u> are <u>smaller</u>, so this
is the most <u>sensible</u> unit.   Millilitre

b) **The mass of a hamster.**

Find the units used to
measure <u>mass</u>.   Gram and kilogram
<u>Grams</u> are <u>smaller</u>, so this
is the most <u>sensible</u> unit.   Gram

Using <u>sensible</u> guesses you can also <u>estimate</u> the <u>measurement</u> of something.

--- Example ---

The man in the picture is 2 m tall. Estimate the height of the tree.

The tree is about <u>one and a half
times</u> as tall as the man.

Rough height of tree = 1.5 × height of man
= 1.5 × 2 m = 3 m

Practice Questions

1) How much
liquid is there
in this jug?

2) Which units from the box would you use to measure:
a) the length of a banana
b) the mass of a horse
c) the flight distance of a jumbo jet?

| mm | cm | tonnes | mg |
| g | km | kg | litres |

Time

There's nothing new here — just a quick reminder about working with time.

> <u>am</u> means <u>morning</u>.
> <u>pm</u> means <u>afternoon or evening</u>.

> <u>12 am</u> (<u>00:00</u>) means <u>midnight</u>.
> <u>12 pm</u> (<u>12:00</u>) means <u>noon</u>.

12-hour clock	24-hour clock
12.00 am	00:00
1.12 am	01:12
12.15 pm	12:15
1.47 pm	13:47
11.32 pm	23:32

The hours on 12- and 24-hour clocks are <u>different after 1 pm</u>. To go from 12-hour to 24-hour <u>add 12 hours</u>, and subtract 12 go the other way.

$$3.24 \text{ pm} \xrightarrow[- 12\text{ h}]{+ 12\text{ h}} 15:24$$

Do **Time** Calculations in **Stages**

— **Example** —

How many minutes are there between 7.20 pm and 10.05 pm?

1) Split the time between 7.20 pm and 10.05 pm into <u>simple stages</u>.

2) <u>Convert</u> the hours to minutes.

3) <u>Add</u> to get the total minutes.

7.20 pm $\xrightarrow{+ 2 \text{ hours}}$ 9.20 pm $\xrightarrow{+ 40 \text{ minutes}}$ 10.00 pm $\xrightarrow{+ 5 \text{ minutes}}$ 10.05 pm

2 hours = 2 × 60 = 120 minutes

120 + 40 + 5 = 165 minutes

> *Be careful when using calculators in time calculations — the decimal answers they give are confusing, e.g. 2.5 hours = 2 hours 30 mins, NOT 2 hours 50 mins.*

— **Example** —

Amy catches the 15:32 bus from Leamington Spa to Bubbenhall. If her journey takes 1 hour and 12 minutes, what time does she arrive?

1) First add on the <u>hour</u>.   15:32 + 1 hour = 16:32

2) Then add on the <u>minutes</u>.   16:32 + 12 minutes = 16:44

Days, Months and Years

Remember, remember the 5th of November. And also all these other facts:

- There are <u>365 days</u>, or <u>12 months</u>, in a <u>year</u>. (But there are 366 days in a leap year.)
- There are <u>10 years</u> in a <u>decade</u>, <u>100 years</u> in a <u>century</u> and <u>1000 years</u> in a <u>millennium</u>.

— **Example** —

How many years and months are there between the 27th November 2010 and 27th July 2014?

1) Count the number of <u>whole years</u> between the two dates.

Nov. 2010 $\xrightarrow{1 \text{ year}}$ Nov. 2011 $\xrightarrow{+ 1 \text{ year}}$ Nov. 2012 $\xrightarrow{+ 1 \text{ year}}$ Nov. 2013 = <u>3 years</u>

2) This takes you to 27th November 2013. 8 months
Now count the number of <u>months</u>.   3 years and 8 months

> 30 days has September, April, June and November. All the rest have 31, except February alone, which has 28 days clear, and 29 in each leap year.

Practice Question

1) Work out how many months and days there are between 23rd April 2014 and 5th August 2014

Maps and Scale Drawings

Scales tell you what a distance on a map or drawing represents in real life. They can be written in different ways, but they all say something like "1 cm represents 5 km".

Map Scales

1 cm = 3 km   — "1 cm represents 3 km"

1 : 2000   — 1 cm on the map means 2000 cm in real life.
        Converting to m gives "1 cm represents 20 m".

⌐————————⌐ Use a ruler — the line's 2 cm long, so 2 cm means 1 km.
0   km   1   Dividing by 2 gives "1 cm represents 0.5 km".

See p.58 for a reminder about conversions.

To <u>convert</u> between <u>maps</u> and <u>real life</u>, <u>learn</u> these rules:

- Make sure your scale is of the form "<u>1 cm = ...</u>"
- To find <u>REAL-LIFE</u> distances, <u>MULTIPLY</u> by the <u>SCALE</u>.
- To find <u>MAP</u> distances, <u>DIVIDE</u> by the <u>SCALE</u>.
- Always check your answer looks <u>sensible</u>.

Scale Drawings

The rules above work for <u>scale drawings</u> too.

Example

This is a scale drawing of Joe's garden. 1 cm represents 2 m.
Find the real length and width of the patio in m.

① Measure with a <u>ruler</u>.   Length on drawing = 3 cm
            Width on drawing = 1.5 cm

② <u>Multiply</u> to get   Real length = 3 × 2 = 6 m
   real-life length.   Real width = 1.5 × 2 = 3 m ← Real life units are in m.

Patio

Compass Directions

Compass points describe the <u>direction</u> of something — <u>learn</u> all <u>8 directions</u> and the bearing from North (see next page) of each one.

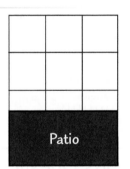

	000° North (N)	
315° North-West (NW)		045° North-East (NE)
270° West (W)		090° East (E)
225° South-West (SW)	180° South (S)	135° South-East (SE)

Example

Cat is standing 10 m north-east of Matt.
Use the scale of 1 cm = 5 m to show where Cat is standing.

N
45°
×Cat
Matt

Take a look at p.78 to see how to use your protractor.

Real-life distance = 10 m, scale is 1 cm = 5 m

<u>Divide</u> for a <u>map distance</u>.

Distance on map = 10 ÷ 5 = <u>2 cm</u>

Use a protractor to mark a <u>bearing</u> of 045° from Matt and draw a line. Then mark Cat's position <u>2 cm</u> along the line.

Practice Question

1) Joe's flower bed measures 2 m by 4 m.
   What would it measure on the scale drawing of his garden above?

Bearings

If you can keep your bearings whilst learning these rules, you'll pick up loads of lovely marks.

Bearings

To find or plot a bearing you must remember <u>the three key words</u>:

The bearing of
A from B

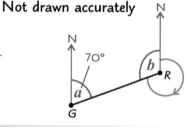

| 1) 'FROM' | <u>Find the word 'FROM' in the question</u>, and put your pencil on the diagram at the point you are going 'from'. |

| 2) <u>NORTHLINE</u> | At the point you are going <u>FROM</u>, draw in a <u>NORTHLINE</u>. |

The northline might have already been drawn in for you.

| 3) <u>CLOCKWISE</u> | Now draw in the angle <u>CLOCKWISE from the northline to the line joining the two points</u>. This angle is the required bearing. |

Example

(L2) Find the bearing of S from T.

| ALL BEARINGS SHOULD BE GIVEN AS 3 FIGURES e.g. 176°, 034° (not 34°), 005° (not 5°), 018° etc. |

1) 'From T'

2) Northline at T

3) Clockwise, from the N-line. This angle is the bearing of <u>S from T</u>. Find the angle using your protractor — 190°.

Example

(L2) The bearing of R from G is 070°. Find the bearing of G from R.

First sketch a diagram so you can see what's going on.
Angles a and b are <u>allied</u>, so they add up to <u>180°</u>.
Angle b = 180° − 70° = 110°
So bearing of G from R = 360° − 110° = 250°.

See page 80 for allied angles.

Not drawn accurately

Bearings Questions and **Scale Drawings**

Example

(L2) A boat is anchored 3 km from point O, on a bearing of 056°. If the scale of the map below is 2 cm to 1 km, how far is the boat now from the pier?

1) First, draw a line at a <u>bearing of 056°</u> from point O. <u>1 km</u> is <u>2 cm</u> on the map and the boat is anchored <u>3 km</u> away from O, so make the line <u>6 cm</u> long and mark the boat.

2) You want the distance of the boat from the pier, so use a ruler to measure it on the map, then use the scale to work out the <u>real distance</u> it represents.

Distance to pier on map = 2 cm.
2 cm = 1 km, so real distance = 1 km.

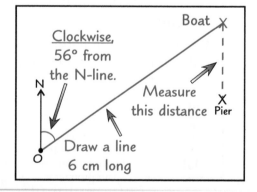

Clockwise, 56° from the N-line.

Measure this distance

Draw a line 6 cm long

Practice Questions

1) Find the bearing of A from B.
(L2) 2) Find the bearing of B from A.

Section 4 — Ratio, Proportion and Rates of Change

Speed

To answer speed, distance and time questions, learn the formula and put in the numbers.

Speed = Distance ÷ Time

Speed is the <u>distance travelled per unit time</u>, e.g. the number of <u>km per hour</u> or <u>metres per second</u>.

$$\text{SPEED} = \frac{\text{DISTANCE}}{\text{TIME}} \qquad \text{TIME} = \frac{\text{DISTANCE}}{\text{SPEED}} \qquad \text{DISTANCE} = \text{SPEED} \times \text{TIME}$$

Here's a handy <u>formula triangle</u> for speed — think of the words <u>SaD Times</u> to help you remember the order of the letters (S^DT).

E.g. to get the formula for <u>speed</u> from the triangle, cover up <u>S</u> and you're left with $\frac{D}{T}$.

HOW DO YOU USE FORMULA TRIANGLES?

1) <u>COVER UP</u> the thing you want to find and <u>WRITE DOWN</u> what's left showing.

2) Now <u>PUT IN THE VALUES</u> for the other two things and <u>WORK IT OUT</u>.

— **Example**

A car travels 90 miles at 60 mph. **How long does this take?**

Write down the <u>formula</u> for <u>time</u>, put in the values and <u>calculate</u>:

$$\text{time} = \frac{\text{distance}}{\text{speed}} = \frac{90 \text{ miles}}{60 \text{ mph}} = 1.5 \text{ hours} = 1 \text{ h } 30 \text{ mins}$$

Find the **Average Speed** of a **Journey** L3

A journey could have lots of <u>different stages</u>. Look at the <u>total time</u> from <u>start</u> to <u>finish</u>, and the <u>total distance</u> travelled. You can use these to work out the <u>average speed</u> for the <u>whole journey</u>.

— **Example**

L3 Dave is doing a sponsored walk. He starts at 9.00 am and walks for 2 hours 45 minutes at 4 km/h. After stopping to rest for 15 minutes, he jogs a further 9 km in 1 hour. Dave then decides to run the remaining 7 km, finishing the walk at 1.30 pm.

a) **How far did Dave walk in the first 2 hours 45 minutes?**

Write down the <u>formula</u> for <u>distance</u>, put in the values and <u>calculate</u>:

distance = speed × time

= 4 km/h × 2.75 hours = 11 km

Convert hours and minutes into a decimal first.

b) **What was Dave's average speed, in km/h, for the whole walk?**

1) Use your answer from part a) to work out his <u>total distance</u> travelled.

11 km + 9 km + 7 km = 27 km

2) Work out the <u>total time</u> from start to finish.

9.00 am _ 1.00 pm _ 1.30 pm
+ 4 hrs   + 30 min = 4 hrs 30 mins
= 4.5 hours

3) Now write down the <u>formula</u> for <u>speed</u>, put in the values and <u>calculate</u>.

$$\text{speed} = \frac{\text{distance}}{\text{time}} = \frac{27 \text{ km}}{4.5 \text{ hours}} = 6 \text{ km/h}$$

Practice Questions

1) Katie runs 5 km in 25 minutes. What is her speed in km/h?

L3 2) Katie then runs 10 km in 35 minutes. What is her average speed for the whole journey?

Section 4 — Ratio, Proportion and Rates of Change

Summary Questions

Just when you thought you were done with section 4, some sneaky revision questions appeared.

- Try these questions and <u>tick off each one</u> when you <u>get it right</u>.
- When you've done <u>all the questions</u> for a topic and are <u>completely happy</u> with it, tick off the topic

(L1) <u>Ratios, Proportion and Percentage Change (p52-57)</u> ☐

1) Reduce these ratios to their simplest form: a) $14:16$ b) $27:18$ c) 56 cm$:0.49$ m
2) Write the ratio $5:18$ in the form $1:n$.
3) (L2) Ria's DVD collection is made up of comedies, dramas and horror films only in the ratio $8:11:6$, and she has 22 dramas. How many DVDs does she have in total?
4) If Isla and Brett share £150 between them in the ratio $7:3$, how much does Isla get?
5) 18 sweets cost 90p. How much would 25 sweets cost?
6) Ben's £200 pogo stick has decreased in price by 65%. How much is it worth now?
7) (L2) If a train ticket increases from £5.00 to £5.80, what is the percentage increase?

(L1) <u>Units and Conversions (p58-60)</u> ☐

8) From memory, write down all the metric unit conversions and all the approximate metric-imperial conversions from page 58.
9) Convert the following: a) 80 km to miles   b) 2.5 feet to cm
10) A giant watermelon weighs 10 kg. What is this in grams?
11) Convert the following: a) 20 cm into m   (L2) b) 6000 mm^2 into cm^2
12) (L2) A matchbox has a volume of 180 cm^3. What is its volume in mm^3?
13) (L2) Charlotte is driving at 27 mph. What is her speed in km/h?

(L1) <u>Reading Scales, Estimating and Time (p61-62)</u> ☑

14) What measurement is the scale on the right showing?
15) What metric units would you use to measure the mass of a kiwi fruit?
16) Estimate the volume of a milk carton. Choose from these options: 1 ml, 1 cl, 1 litre.
17) How many minutes are there between 6.40 pm and 11.20 pm?

(L1) <u>Maps, Scale Drawings and Bearings (p63-64)</u> ☐

18) The distance between two towns is 20 miles.
    How far apart would they be on a map with a scale of 1 cm$:5$ miles?
19) On a scale drawing, the dimensions of a car park are 5 cm by 2.5 cm.
    The scale is 1 cm = 10 m. What are the real-life dimensions of the car park?
20) Draw a compass and label all 8 points.
21) Use the diagram on the right to work out the bearing of D from C.
22) (L2) Use the diagram on the right to work out the bearing of C from D.

(L2) <u>Speed (p65)</u> ☐

23) Ramin cycles for 3 hours at a speed of 25 km/h. How far does he cycle?
24) A tricycle takes 45 minutes to travel 3 km. How fast does it travel?
25) (L3) Ben rows 2 km in 30 minutes. The wind changes direction, and he rows a further 3 km at 10 km/h. What is his average speed for the whole distance he rows?

Section 4 — Ratio, Proportion and Rates of Change

Symmetry

There are two types of <u>symmetry</u> you need to know — <u>line symmetry</u> and <u>rotational symmetry</u>.

Line Symmetry

This is where you draw one or more <u>MIRROR LINES</u> across a shape and both sides will <u>fold exactly</u> together.

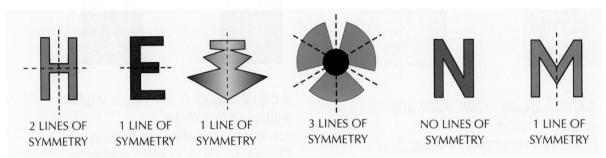

| 2 LINES OF SYMMETRY | 1 LINE OF SYMMETRY | 1 LINE OF SYMMETRY | 3 LINES OF SYMMETRY | NO LINES OF SYMMETRY | 1 LINE OF SYMMETRY |

Example

Shade two squares on the pattern on the right to make a pattern with two lines of symmetry, and draw on the lines of symmetry.

The extra squares are shown in blue.

These are the lines of symmetry

Rotational Symmetry

This is where you can <u>rotate</u> the shape into different positions that <u>look exactly the same</u>.

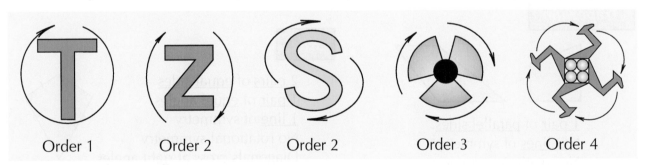

| Order 1 | Order 2 | Order 2 | Order 3 | Order 4 |

The <u>ORDER OF ROTATIONAL SYMMETRY</u> is the posh way of saying: 'how many different positions look the same'. You should say the Z-shape above has '<u>rotational symmetry of order 2</u>'.

> When a shape has <u>only 1 position</u> you can <u>either</u> say that it has 'rotational symmetry of <u>order 1</u>' <u>or</u> that it has '<u>NO rotational symmetry</u>'.

Practice Questions

1) How many lines of symmetry does the T-shape above have?
2) What is the order of rotational symmetry of the H-shape above?

Quadrilaterals

This page is full of quadrilateral facts that you'll need to learn.

Quadrilaterals (Four-Sided Shapes)

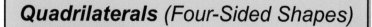

Rectangle

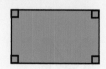

4 equal angles of 90° (right angles)
2 lines of symmetry
rotational symmetry of order 2

Square

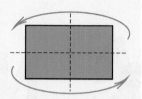

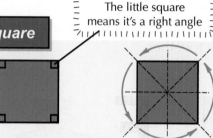

The little square means it's a right angle

4 equal angles of 90° (right angles)
4 lines of symmetry,
rotational symmetry of order 4
Diagonals cross at right angles

Parallelogram (a rectangle pushed over)

2 pairs of equal sides
(each pair are parallel)
2 pairs of equal angles
NO lines of symmetry,
rotational symmetry of order 2

Rhombus (a square pushed over)

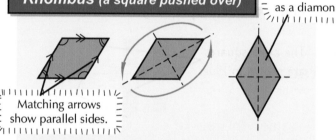

A rhombus is the same as a diamond

Matching arrows show parallel sides.

4 equal sides (opposite sides are parallel)
2 pairs of equal angles
2 lines of symmetry,
rotational symmetry of order 2
Diagonals cross at right angles

Trapezium

1 pair of parallel sides.
NO lines of symmetry*
No rotational symmetry

Kite

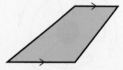

2 pairs of equal sides
1 pair of equal angles
1 line of symmetry
No rotational symmetry
Diagonals cross at right angles

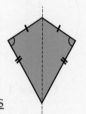

*except for an isosceles trapezium (a trapezium where the non-parallel
sides are the same length), which has 1 line of symmetry.

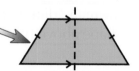

Practice Question

1) I am thinking of a shape with four sides. It has 2 pairs of equal sides and its diagonals cross at right angles. It has no rotational symmetry. What is the name of the shape I'm thinking of?

Triangles and Regular Polygons

There are some more 2D shapes coming up on this page — let's start off with triangles.

Triangles *(Three-Sided Shapes)*

Equilateral Triangles

3 equal sides and
3 equal angles of 60°
3 lines of symmetry,
rotational symmetry
of order 3 (see p.67)

Right-Angled Triangles

1 right angle (90°)
No lines of symmetry

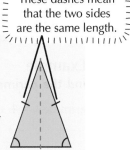

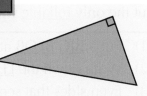
These dashes mean
that the two sides
are the same length.

Scalene Triangles

All three sides different
All three angles different
No symmetry (pretty obviously)

Isosceles Triangles

2 sides the same
2 angles the same
1 line of symmetry
No rotational symmetry

Regular Polygons

A polygon is a many-sided shape. A regular polygon is one where all the sides and angles are the same. The regular polygons are a never-ending series of shapes with some fancy features.

EQUILATERAL TRIANGLE
3 sides
3 lines of symmetry
Rotational symmetry of order 3

SQUARE
4 sides
4 lines of symmetry
Rotational symmetry of order 4

REGULAR PENTAGON
5 sides
5 lines of symmetry
Rotational symmetry of order 5

REGULAR HEXAGON
6 sides
6 lines of symmetry
Rotational symmetry of order 6

REGULAR HEPTAGON
7 sides
7 lines of symmetry
Rotational symmetry of order 7
(A 50p piece is like a heptagon.)

REGULAR OCTAGON
8 sides
8 lines of symmetry
Rotational symmetry of order 8

REGULAR NONAGON
9 sides
9 lines of symmetry
Rotational symmetry of order 9

REGULAR DECAGON
10 sides
10 lines of symmetry
Rotational symmetry of order 10

Practice Question

1) A regular polygon has 20 sides. How many lines of symmetry does it have?
   What is its order of rotational symmetry?

Perimeter and Area

Finding the perimeter is pretty straightforward if you use the big blob method.

Perimeter — Distance Around the Edge of a Shape

To find a <u>perimeter</u>, you <u>add up</u> the <u>lengths</u> of all the sides,
but the only <u>reliable</u> way to make sure you get <u>all</u> the sides is this:

1) Put a <u>BIG BLOB</u> at one corner and then go around the shape.
2) Write down the <u>LENGTH</u> of every side as you go along.
3) Even sides that seem to have <u>NO LENGTH GIVEN</u> — you must <u>work them out</u>.
4) Keep going until you get back to the <u>BIG BLOB</u>.
5) <u>ADD UP</u> all the lengths you've written down.

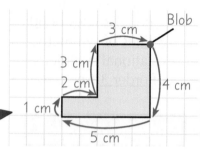

Example

Find the perimeter of the shape drawn on the grid. Each grid square represents 1 cm².

Perimeter = 4 + 5 + 1 + 2 + 3 + 3 = 18 cm

Three Area Formulas

At Level 1, you'll be given a formula sheet with these on, but you should still learn how they're used.

Area of <u>RECTANGLE</u> = length × width

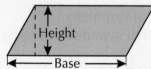

Width
Length

$A = l \times w$

Area of <u>TRIANGLE</u> = $\frac{1}{2}$ × base × vertical height

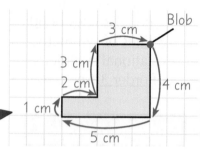

Height
Base

$A = \frac{1}{2} \times b \times h$

Area of <u>PARALLELOGRAM</u> = base × vertical height

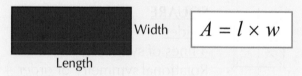

Height
Base

$A = b \times h$

1) <u>Height</u> always means the <u>vertical height</u>, not the sloping height.
2) Remember that area is <u>measured</u> in <u>square units</u> (e.g. cm², m² or km²).

Example

Find the area of triangle A.

Use the formula:

Area = $\frac{1}{2}$ × 18 × 12 = 9 × 12 = 108 cm²

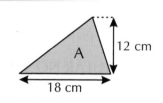

A
12 cm
18 cm

Practice Questions

1) A rectangle has a perimeter of 14 m, and an area of 12 m². Write down all its side lengths.
2) Find the area of a parallelogram with a base of 8 cm and a height of 5 cm using the formula $A = b \times h$.

Area of Compound Shapes

Make sure you know how to find the area of different shapes — you'll need to do it again here.

Areas of *More Complicated* Shapes

You sometimes have to find the area of <u>strange-looking</u> shapes. What you always find with these questions is that you can break the shape up into <u>simpler ones</u> that you can deal with.

> 1) <u>SPLIT THEM UP</u> into the basic shapes: <u>RECTANGLES</u>, <u>TRIANGLES</u>, etc.
> 2) Work out the area of each bit <u>SEPARATELY</u>.
> 3) Then <u>ADD THEM ALL TOGETHER</u>.

Example

The shape of a symmetrical school badge is shown on the right.
Find the area of the badge.

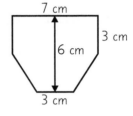

1) You need to work out the <u>area</u> of the badge —
   so split it into two shapes (a <u>rectangle</u> and a <u>trapezium</u>):

2) Find the area of the <u>rectangle</u>:
   Area = *l* × *w* = 7 × 3 = 21 cm²

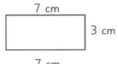

3) Split the trapezium up into
   <u>2 identical triangles</u> and a <u>square</u>.

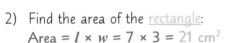

4) Find the area of each triangle.
   Area of each triangle = $\frac{1}{2}$ × 2 × 3 = 3 cm²

5) Find the area of the square.
   Area of square = 3 × 3 = 9 cm²

6) Add up all the parts to find the total area.
   The <u>total area</u> of the badge is 21 + 9 + 3 + 3 = 36 cm²

Example

 Mollie has a parallelogram-shaped pond in her garden. If the shaded area of the
diagram represents grass, calculate the area of the grass Mollie has in her garden.

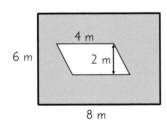

1) Find the area of the <u>whole garden</u>:
   Area = *l* × *w* = 8 × 6 = 48 m²

2) Find the area of the <u>pond</u>:
   Area of parallelogram = *b* × *h* = 4 × 2 = 8 m²

3) <u>Subtract</u> the pond area from the garden area.
   Area of grass = 48 − 8 = 40 m²

Practice Question

As long as you know the area formulas, there's nothing on this page to trip you up. Here's a question to see if you've got it all down.

1) Find the area of the shape on the right.

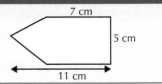

Section 5 — Geometry and Measures

Circles

There's a surprising number of circle terms you need to know — don't mix them up.

Radius and *Diameter*

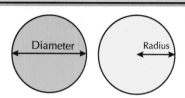

The <u>DIAMETER</u> goes <u>right across</u> the circle, passing through the <u>centre</u>.
The <u>RADIUS</u> goes from the <u>centre</u> of the circle to any point on the <u>edge</u>.

The <u>DIAMETER IS EXACTLY DOUBLE THE RADIUS</u>

> E.g. if the radius is 4 cm, the diameter is 8 cm,
> and if the diameter is 24 m, the radius is 12 m.

Area, Circumference and π

There are two more important formulas for you to <u>learn</u> — circumference and area of a circle.
The circumference is the distance round the outside of the circle (its <u>perimeter</u>).

1) <u>CIRCUMFERENCE</u> $= \pi \times$ diameter
$= \pi \times$ radius $\times 2$

$$C = \pi \times D \ \text{ or } \ C = 2 \times \pi \times r$$

2) <u>AREA</u> $= \pi \times$ (radius)^2

$$A = \pi \times r^2$$

$\pi = 3.141592.... = \underline{3.142}$ (approx)

The big thing to remember is that π (called "pi")
is just an <u>ordinary number</u> equal to 3.14159... or
3.142 rounded off. You can just use the π button
on your calculator (which is way more accurate).

So a circle with radius <u>4 cm</u> has a <u>circumference</u> of $2 \times \pi \times r = 2 \times \pi \times 4 = \underline{25.1 \text{ cm}}$ (1 d.p.)
and an <u>area</u> of $\pi \times r^2 = \pi \times 4^2 = \underline{50.3 \text{ cm}^2}$ (1 d.p.).

Finding the Radius or Diameter

You could be given the <u>circumference</u> or the <u>area</u> of a circle and asked
to find the <u>radius</u> or <u>diameter</u>. You do this by <u>using</u> the formulas above.

— **Example** —

 A circle has a circumference of 37.7 cm. What is its radius?
Write your answer to the nearest whole number.

1) Write out the formula for <u>circumference</u>. $\quad C = 2 \times \pi \times r$

2) <u>Substitute</u> the values that you know... $\quad 37.7 = 2 \times \pi \times r$

3) ...and <u>solve</u> to calculate r. $\quad r = \frac{37.7}{2\pi} = 6.00014... = 6$ cm

Practice Questions

1) Find the circumference and area (to 1 d.p.) of a circle with a diameter of 20 mm.

2) A circle has an area of 60 cm². Give its diameter to 3 significant figures.

Circle Problems

Here's some more circle stuff to get your head around.

Tangents, Chords, Arcs, Sectors and Segments

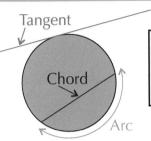

A TANGENT is a straight line that just touches the outside of a circle.
A CHORD is a line drawn across the inside of a circle.
AN ARC is just part of the circumference of a circle.

A SECTOR is a wedge-shaped area (like a slice of cake) cut right from the centre.
SEGMENTS are the areas you get when you cut a circle with a chord.

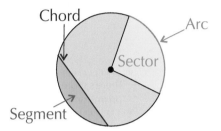

Finding the Area of a Sector

Finding the area of a sector can be a bit tricky — but there's a handy formula to help.

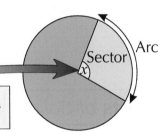

$$\text{AREA OF SECTOR} = \frac{x}{360} \times \text{Area of Full Circle}$$

Example

Nick cuts a slice from a circular pizza with a radius of 9 cm.
The pizza remaining is shown in the diagram.
Work out the area of the remaining pizza to 1 d.p.

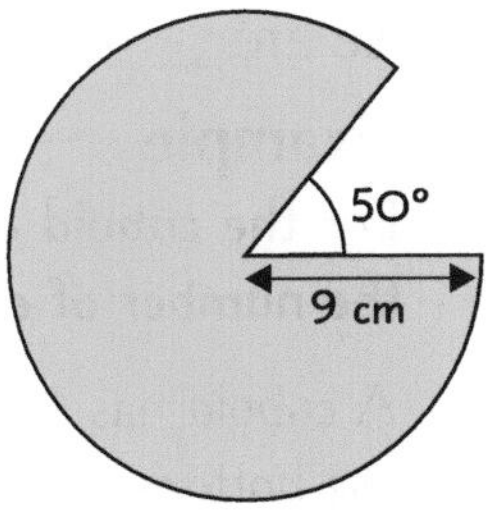

1) Start by working out the area of the circle.

$A = \pi \times r^2 = \pi \times 9^2$
$= \underline{254.469...} \text{ cm}^2$

2) Now work out the area of the missing sector (the slice that's been removed).

Area of sector $= \frac{50}{360} \times 254.469... = \underline{35.342...} \text{ cm}^2$

3) Subtract the area of the sector from the circle...

$254.469... - 35.342... = 219.126... \text{ cm}^2$

4) ...and round your answer to 1 d.p.

So area of remaining pizza $= 219.1 \text{ cm}^2$ to 1 d.p.

Practice Questions

1) Draw and label a circle with a chord, tangent and segment.

2) Find the area of the shape to the right.
Give your answer to 2 d.p.

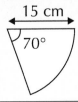

15 cm

70°

3) Work out the shaded area below.
Give your answer to 1 d.p.

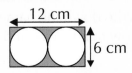

12 cm

6 cm

Section 5 — Geometry and Measures

3D Shapes

3D shapes can be quite complicated, but luckily you don't need to know anything too tricky.

Eight **Solids** to Learn

3D shapes are solid shapes. These are some of the more common ones:

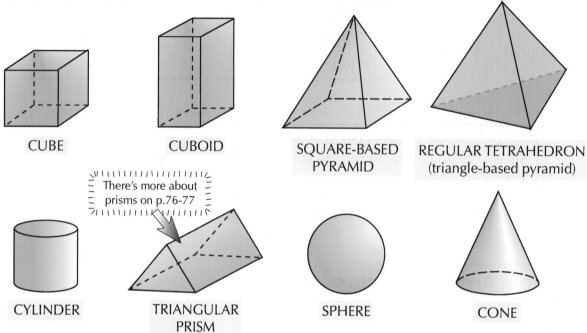

CUBE CUBOID SQUARE-BASED PYRAMID REGULAR TETRAHEDRON (triangle-based pyramid)

There's more about prisms on p.76-77

CYLINDER TRIANGULAR PRISM SPHERE CONE

Different Parts of Solids

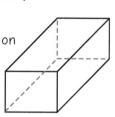

Vertex Face Edge

There are different parts of 3D shapes to know about.
These are vertices (corners), faces (the flat bits) and edges.

— **Example** —

For the cuboid on the right, write down the number of faces, the number of edges and the number of vertices.

A cuboid has **6 faces** (don't forget the hidden faces — one on the bottom and two at the back shown by the dotted lines).

It has **12 edges** (again, there are some hidden ones — the dotted lines in the diagram).

It has **8 vertices** (one is hidden).

— **Example** —

Write down the number of faces on a triangular prism.
A triangular prism has **5 faces** (there's one on the bottom and two at the back that you can't see).

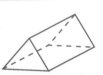

Practice Question

1) a) Write down the name of the shape on the right.
   b) How many faces and edges does it have?

Nets and Surface Area

Pencils and rulers at the ready — you might get to do some drawing over the next two pages.

Nets and Surface Area

1) A NET is just a hollow 3D shape folded out flat.
2) There's often more than one net that can be drawn for a 3D shape (see the cubes below).
3) If you're given a net, you can fold it up to make a 3D shape.
4) SURFACE AREA only applies to 3D objects — it's the total area of all the faces added together.
5) To find the surface area, sketch the net, then find the area of the net.

Remember — SURFACE AREA OF SOLID = AREA OF NET.

These are just some of the nets of a cube — there are lots more.

Cubes

Nets of Cubes

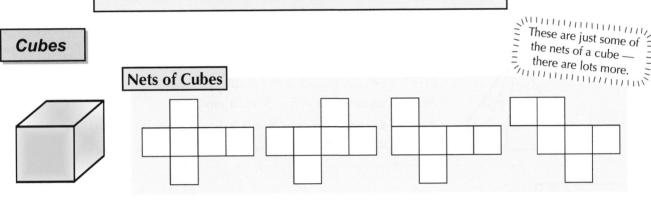

Cuboids

Net of cuboid

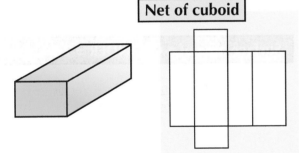

Notice that the net of a cuboid is made up of 3 different sized rectangles (there are 2 of each size). This is helpful when you're working out the surface area.

Example

Find the surface area of this cuboid:

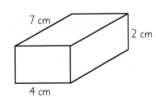

Sketch the net of the shape, and label all the measurements:

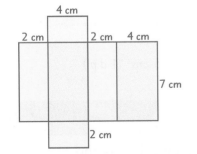

Then work out the area of each face and add them up (note there are 2 each of 3 different rectangles).

Surface area = 2(2 × 7) + 2(4 × 7) + 2(4 × 2)
= 28 + 56 + 16 = 100 cm²

Practice Question

1) Find the surface area of a cube with side length 4 cm.

Nets and Surface Area

Another page on nets and surface area — it's time for prisms, pyramids and cylinders.

Prisms and Pyramids

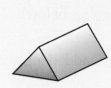 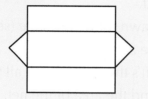 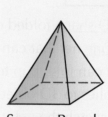 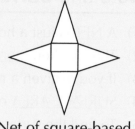

Triangular Prism | Net of triangular prism

Square-Based Pyramid | Net of square-based pyramid

Example

Find the surface area of the square-based pyramid below.

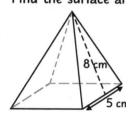

You can see from the <u>net</u> above that a square-based pyramid has <u>1 square face</u> and <u>4 triangular faces</u>.

Area of square face = 5 × 5 = 25 cm²

Area of triangular face = ½ × 5 × 8 = 20 cm²

Total surface area = 25 + (4 × 20) = 25 + 80 = 105 cm²

Have a look back at p.70 for more on areas.

Cylinders L3

<u>Cylinders</u> are a bit trickier — it's probably best to just <u>learn the formula</u> and stick the numbers in.

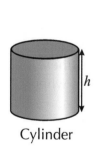

Cylinder

πr^2

$2\pi r$

Net of cylinder

πr^2

Surface area of a CYLINDER = $2\pi rh + 2\pi r^2$

Note that <u>the length of the rectangle</u> is equal to the <u>circumference</u> of the circular ends.

Example

Find the surface area of the cylinder below to 1 d.p.

Just put the <u>measurements</u> into the <u>formula</u>:

Surface area of cylinder = $2\pi rh + 2\pi r^2$

$= (2 \times \pi \times 2 \times 6) + (2 \times \pi \times 2^2)$

$= 75.398... + 25.132...$

$= 100.530... = 100.5$ cm² (1 d.p.)

Practice Questions

You have to be a bit careful when finding the surface area of a triangular prism — the rectangles will be different sizes (unless the triangle is equilateral), so don't get caught out.

1) Draw the net of a pentagon-based pyramid.
2) What is the surface area of the regular tetrahedron shown, given that area A = 3 cm²?

Section 5 — Geometry and Measures

Volume

Now it's time to work out the volumes of 3D shapes.

Volumes of Cuboids

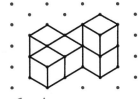

A <u>cuboid</u> is a <u>rectangular block</u>. Finding its volume is dead easy:

Height

Width

Length

| Volume of a Cuboid = length × width × height | $V = l \times w \times h$ |

You can count the number of cubes in a shape to find the volume, or use the formula above.

Examples

In the diagram, each cube has a volume of 1 cm³. What is the volume of the whole shape?

1) Count the number of cubes. 6 cubes
2) Multiply the number of cubes $6 \times 1 \text{ cm}^3 = 6 \text{ cm}^3$ by the volume of each cube.

Find the volume of a cuboid with a length of 5 cm, a width of 7 cm and a height of 9 cm.

Use the <u>formula</u> $V = l \times w \times h$
for volume and $= 5 \times 7 \times 9$
plug in the values. $= 315 \text{ cm}^3$

Don't forget your units — it'll always be 'something-cubed'.

Volumes of Prisms and Cylinders

A PRISM is a solid (3D) object which is the same shape all the way through — i.e. it has a CONSTANT AREA OF CROSS-SECTION.

Triangular Prism

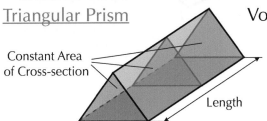

Constant Area of Cross-section

Length

Volume of Prism = cross-sectional area × length

$V = A \times L$

Prisms are sometimes called 'right prisms'.

Cylinder

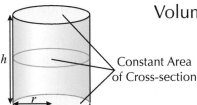

h

Constant Area of Cross-section

r

Volume of Cylinder = area of circle × height

$V = \pi r^2 h$

Cylinders are sometimes called 'right cylinders'.

Example

Rufus has a cylindrical jar of jam with radius 3 cm and height 10 cm. What is the volume of the jar to 3 s.f.?

Just put the measurements into the <u>formula</u> above:

$V = \pi r^2 h = \pi \times 3^2 \times 10 = 282.743... \text{ cm}^3 = 283 \text{ cm}^3$ (3 s.f.)

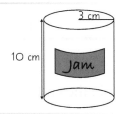

3 cm

10 cm

Jam

Practice Question

1) The cross-sectional area of an octagonal prism is 28 cm². The length of the prism is 6 cm. Find the volume of the prism.

Angle Basics

Here's a page to ease you into the world of all things angles.

Fancy **Angle Names**

Some angles have special names which you need to know.

Acute angles

Sharp pointy ones
(less than 90°)

Right angles

Square corners
(exactly 90°)

Obtuse angles

Flatter ones
(between 90° and 180°)

Reflex angles

Ones that bend
back on themselves
(more than 180°)

Three-Letter Angle Notation

The best way to say which angle you're talking about in a diagram is by using THREE letters.
For example in the diagram, angle $BAC = 35°$.

1) The middle letter is where the angle is.
2) The other two letters tell you which two lines enclose the angle.

 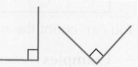 

NOT TO SCALE

B

$25°$ C

$35°$ $20°$

A angle $ACD = 20°$

$30°$

D

You might see angles written
in other ways as well —
$\angle ABC$ and $A\hat{B}C$ are both
the same as angle ABC.

Drawing Angles with a **Protractor**

Draw a straight horizontal line to be your base line. Put the protractor on the line so that the middle of the protractor is on one end of the line as shown:

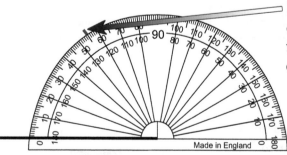

Made in England

Draw a little line or dot next to the angle you're drawing (count up in tens from 0° to make sure you follow the right scale). Here, I'm drawing an angle of 55°, so I'm using the outside scale.

Be careful — reading from the wrong
scale is a very very common error.

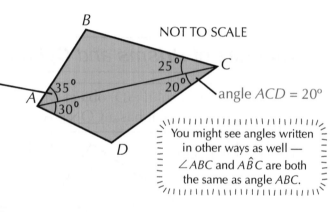

Then join your base line to the mark you've just made with a straight line.
You must join the end of the base line that was in the middle of the protractor.

55°

Practice Question

Make sure you learn all the different angle names, and know how to use your protractor.

1) Write down the names of the following angles: a) 98°   b) 234°   c) 11°.

Geometry Rules

The angle rules on this page are really important — so make sure you learn them all.

6 Simple Rules — that's all

1) Angles in a triangle add up to 180°.

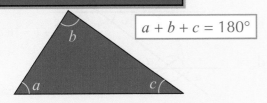

$$a + b + c = 180°$$

2) Angles on a straight line add up to 180°.

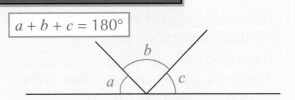

$$a + b + c = 180°$$

3) Angles in a quadrilateral add up to 360°.

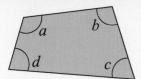

Remember that a quadrilateral is a 4-sided shape.

$$a + b + c + d = 360°$$

4) Angles round a point add up to 360°.

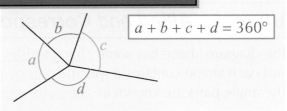

$$a + b + c + d = 360°$$

5) Exterior angle of a triangle = sum of opposite interior angles.

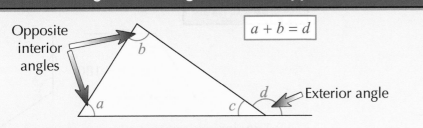

$$a + b = d$$

Opposite interior angles

d Exterior angle

6) Isosceles triangles have 2 sides the same and 2 angles the same.

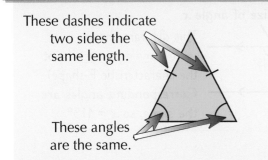

These dashes indicate two sides the same length.

These angles are the same.

In an isosceles triangle, you only need to know one angle to be able to find the other two.

Example

Find the size of angle x.

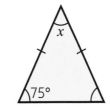

The two angles at the bottom are <u>the same</u> (they're both 75°), so
$$75° + 75° + x = 180°$$
$$x = 180° - 150°$$
$$x = 30°$$

Practice Question

None of the rules here are particularly difficult, but make sure you don't get them mixed up. Once you're happy with them all, have a go at this question.

1) Find the size of angle x in the diagram on the right.

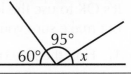

Intersecting and Parallel Lines

Parallel lines are always the same distance apart (and never meet).
Perpendicular lines are always at right angles to each other (they meet at 90°).

Perpendicular line

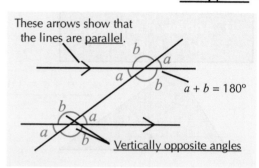

Angles Around **Parallel Lines**

When a line <u>intersects</u> two <u>parallel lines</u>,
it forms special sets of angles.

1) The two <u>bunches</u> of angles formed at the
points of intersection <u>are the same</u>.

2) There are only actually <u>two different angles</u> involved
(labelled *a* and *b* here), and they add up to <u>180°</u>
(from rule 2 on page 79).

3) <u>Vertically opposite angles</u> (ones opposite each other) are <u>equal</u>
(in the diagram, *a* and *a* are vertically opposite, as are *b* and *b*).

These arrows show that
the lines are <u>parallel</u>.

$a + b = 180°$

Vertically opposite angles

Alternate, **Allied** and **Corresponding** Angles

The diagram above has some <u>characteristic shapes</u> to look out for —
and each shape contains a specific <u>pair of angles</u>.
The angle pairs are known as <u>alternate</u>, <u>allied</u> and <u>corresponding angles</u>.

You need to spot the <u>characteristic Z, C, U and F shapes</u>:

ALTERNATE ANGLES

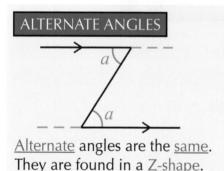

<u>Alternate</u> angles are the <u>same</u>.
They are found in a <u>Z-shape</u>.

ALLIED ANGLES

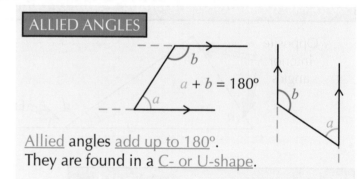

$a + b = 180°$

<u>Allied</u> angles <u>add up to 180°</u>.
They are found in a <u>C- or U-shape</u>.

CORRESPONDING ANGLES

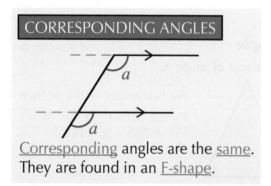

<u>Corresponding</u> angles are the <u>same</u>.
They are found in an <u>F-shape</u>.

— **Example** —

Find the size of angle *x*.

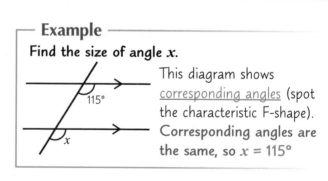

This diagram shows
<u>corresponding angles</u> (spot
the characteristic F-shape).
Corresponding angles are
the same, so *x* = 115°

Practice Question

It's OK to use the letters Z, C, U and F to help you identify the angles,
but make sure you know the proper names too.

1) Find the size of angle *y* in the diagram on the right.

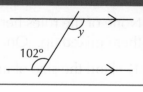

Geometry Problems

Now it's time to put your knowledge to use, and solve some geometry problems.

Try Out **All the Rules** One by One

1) If you're stuck, <u>don't</u> concentrate too much on the angle you have been asked to find.
   Find <u>ALL</u> the angles in <u>whatever order</u> they become obvious.

2) <u>Don't</u> sit there waiting for inspiration to hit you. It's all too easy to find yourself staring
   at a geometry problem and <u>getting nowhere</u>. The method is this:

> <u>GO THROUGH ALL THE RULES OF GEOMETRY</u> (including <u>PARALLEL LINES</u>), <u>ONE BY ONE</u>,
> and apply each of them in turn <u>in as many ways as possible</u> — one of them is bound to work.

Example

Find the size of angle x.

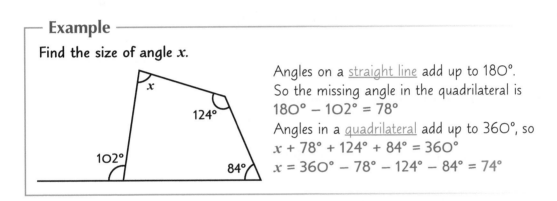

Angles on a <u>straight line</u> add up to 180°.
So the missing angle in the quadrilateral is
180° − 102° = 78°
Angles in a <u>quadrilateral</u> add up to 360°, so
x + 78° + 124° + 84° = 360°
x = 360° − 78° − 124° − 84° = 74°

Example

Find the size of angle x. Give a reason for each step of your working.

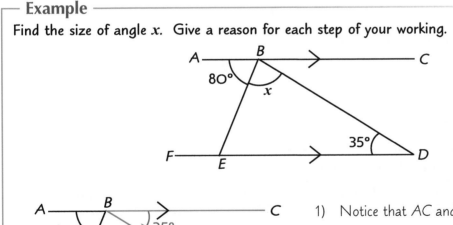

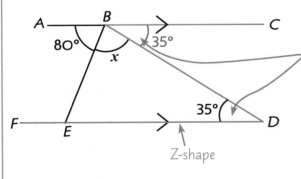

1) Notice that AC and FD are <u>parallel</u>.
   CBD and BDE are alternate angles.
   So CBD = 35°

2) Now you know <u>two angles</u> on straight line AC.
   Angles on a straight line add up to 180°.
   So x = 180° − 80° − 35°
   = 65°

Practice Question

1) Find the size of angle BEF in the diagram above.

Exterior and Interior Angles

You're not quite done with angles yet (sorry) — now it's time for angles in polygons.

Exterior and *Interior* Angles

You need to know <u>what</u> exterior and interior angles in polygons are and <u>how to find them</u>.

For <u>ANY POLYGON</u> (regular or irregular):

| SUM OF EXTERIOR ANGLES = 360° |

| INTERIOR ANGLE = 180° – EXTERIOR ANGLE |

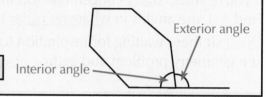

Interior angle —

For <u>REGULAR POLYGONS</u>:

| EXTERIOR ANGLE = $\dfrac{360°}{n}$ | (n is the number of sides) |

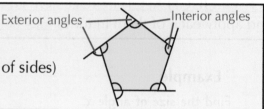

Exterior angles — / Interior angles

Examples

Find the exterior and interior angles of a regular hexagon.

Hexagons have 6 sides: exterior angle = $\dfrac{360°}{n} = \dfrac{360°}{6} = 60°$

Use the exterior angle to find the interior angle: interior angle = 180° – exterior angle

= 180° – 60° = 120°

What regular polygon has exterior angles of 72°?

1) Put 72° into the formula 'exterior angle = $\dfrac{360°}{n}$'. $72° = \dfrac{360°}{n}$

2) Rearrange the equation and do the division to work out the <u>number of sides</u>. $n = \dfrac{360°}{72°} = 5$

Regular pentagon

Sum of *Interior* Angles

For <u>ANY POLYGON</u> (regular or irregular):

| SUM OF INTERIOR ANGLES = $(n – 2) × 180°$ | (n is the number of sides) |

Example

Find the value of x in the diagram on the right.

1) First, find the <u>sum of the interior angles</u> of the 7-sided shape:
    Sum of interior angles = (n – 2) × 180°
    = (7 – 2) × 180° = 900°

2) Now write an <u>equation</u> and <u>solve it</u> to find x:
    x + 170° + 95° + 115° + 100° + 120° + 140° = 900°
    x = 900° – 170° – 95° – 115° – 100° – 120° – 140° = 160°

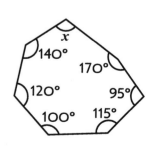

Practice Question

1) Work out the size of an exterior angle and an interior angle of a regular octagon.

Transactions

The next few pages are all about transformations — translation, reflection, rotation, enlargement.

1) Translations

A translation is just a <u>SLIDE</u> around the page. When describing a translation, you must say <u>how far right or left</u> and <u>how far up or down</u> the shape moves.

Examples

Translate square A 3 units right and 2 units up. Label it 'B'.

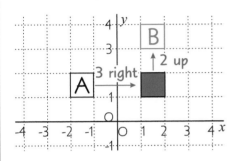

Follow the instructions:

1) Move the square <u>3 places</u> to the <u>right</u>...

2) ...and then <u>2 places up</u>.

Describe the transformation that maps:

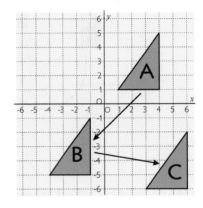

a) triangle A onto triangle B.

To get from triangle A to triangle B you need to move **5 units left** and **6 units down**.

b) triangle B onto triangle C.

Move triangle B **7 units right** and **1 unit down**.

2) Reflections

⌐ See p.44 for more on straight lines. ⌐

Triangle D is mapped onto triangle E by a <u>reflection</u> in the line $x = 1$. Notice that the matching corners are <u>equal distances</u> from the mirror line.
To describe a <u>reflection</u>, you must give the <u>equation</u> of the <u>mirror line</u>.

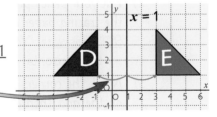

Example

Describe the transformation that maps:

a) Shape F onto shape G.
A reflection in the x-axis

b) Shape G onto shape H.
A reflection in the line $y = x$

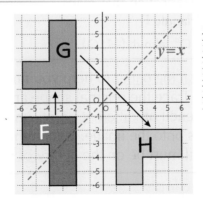

⌐ Any shape that is a <u>translation</u>, <u>reflection</u> or <u>rotation</u> is congruent to the original shape. <u>Congruent</u> shapes are the same <u>shape</u> and <u>size</u>. ⌐

Practice Question

Remember what information you have to give for each transformation — for a translation, you need to give instructions, and for a reflection, you need to give the equation of the mirror line.

1) Describe the transformation that maps triangle A onto triangle C in the diagram above.

Transformations

Transformation number 3 coming up — rotation.

3) Rotations

To describe a rotation, you need 3 details:

1) The angle of rotation (usually 90° or 180°).
2) The direction of rotation (clockwise or anticlockwise).
3) The centre of rotation

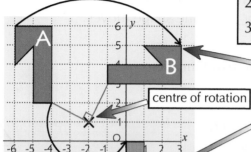

Shape A is mapped onto Shape B by a rotation of 90° clockwise about point (−2, 1).

Shape A is mapped onto Shape C by a rotation of 180° about point (−2, 1).

For a rotation of 180°, it doesn't matter whether you go clockwise or anticlockwise.

You could be asked about quarter turns or half turns — a quarter turn is just a 90° turn, and a half turn is just a 180° turn. Easy.

Example

Rotate Triangle D a quarter turn clockwise about (0, 0).

The best way to tackle this is with tracing paper:

1) Trace the shape and mark the centre of rotation at (0, 0).

2) Put your pencil point on the centre of rotation and rotate the tracing paper a quarter turn clockwise — that's 90° clockwise. You'll know when you've gone far enough — the horizontal side will be vertical, and vice versa.

3) Mark the corners of the shape in their new positions on the grid, then draw the shape.

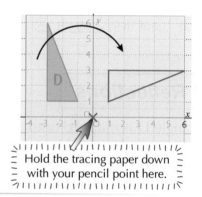

Hold the tracing paper down with your pencil point here.

Example

Describe the transformation that maps Triangle E onto Triangle F.

A half turn, or 180°, about (−1, 0).

You can use tracing paper to help you find the centre of rotation. Trace the original shape and then try putting your pencil on different points until the traced shape rotates onto the image. When this happens your pencil must be on the centre of rotation.

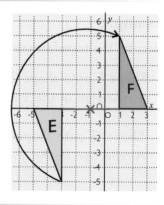

Practice Questions

1) Square S has side length 1 unit and its bottom-left corner is at the coordinates (2, 3).
   a) Draw square S.   b) Rotate square S 180° about (0, 1) and label it T.

2) Triangle G has corners (−3, 2), (−3, 4) and (−8, 2). Draw triangles F (above) and G on a graph, and describe the rotation that maps triangle F onto triangle G.

Transformations

You've made it to the final transformation now — get ready for enlargements.

4) Enlargements

The <u>scale factor</u> for an enlargement tells you <u>how long</u> the sides of the new shape are compared to the old shape. E.g. a scale factor of 3 means you <u>multiply</u> each side length by 3
The <u>centre of enlargement</u> tells you where to start your enlargement from.

> **Example**
>
> **Enlarge shape X by a scale factor of 2 with centre of enlargement C.**
>
> Start by finding where one corner will go — <u>draw a line</u> from C to the bottom-left of X, and then draw the same length <u>again</u>.
> Do the same for <u>every</u> corner and <u>join up</u> the points.
> Each side will be <u>twice as long</u> as the matching side on shape X.
>
>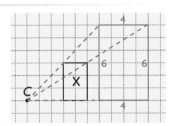

The <u>area</u> of an enlarged shape has the area of the <u>original shape</u> multiplied by the scale factor <u>squared</u>.

> **Example**
>
> **The area of a triangle is 5 cm². It is then enlarged by a scale factor of 3**
> **What is the area of the enlarged triangle?**
>
> Multiply the <u>original area</u> by the <u>scale factor squared</u>.　　　$5 \times 3^2 = 5 \times 9 = 45$ cm²

Describing an Enlargement

To DESCRIBE an <u>ENLARGEMENT</u>, you need:

1) The <u>scale factor</u>. 　　⟶　　$\text{scale factor} = \dfrac{\text{new length}}{\text{old length}}$

2) The <u>centre of enlargement</u>.

> **Example**
>
> **Describe the transformation that maps Triangle A onto Triangle B.**
>
> Use the formula to find the <u>scale factor</u>. (Just do this for one pair of sides.)
>
> Old length of triangle base = 4 units
> New length of triangle base = 2 units
>
> $\text{scale factor} = \dfrac{\text{new length}}{\text{old length}} = \dfrac{2}{4} = \dfrac{1}{2}$
>
> To find the <u>centre of enlargement</u>, draw <u>lines</u> that go through <u>matching corners</u> of both shapes and see where they <u>cross</u>.
>
> So the transformation is an enlargement of scale factor $\frac{1}{2}$, centre (O, 6).
>
>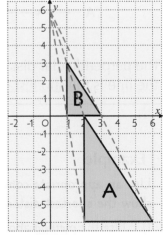
>
> Enlargements give <u>similar shapes</u> — shapes that look the same but are different sizes.

Practice Question

1) Plot the triangles X (1, 2), (−1, 3), (−1, 5) and Y (7, −4), (1, −1), (1, 5) and work out the scale factor for the transformation that maps triangle X onto triangle Y.

Constructions

Here are some <u>constructions</u> that you'll need to be able to do.

The **Perpendicular Bisector** of a **Line**

The perpendicular bisector of line segment AB is a line at <u>right angles</u> to AB, passing through the <u>midpoint</u> of AB. This is the method to use if you're asked to draw it.

Keep the compass setting <u>the same</u> for all of these construction arcs.

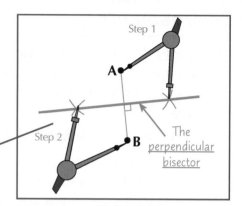

The **Bisector** of an **Angle**

1) Keep the compass setting <u>THE SAME</u> while you make <u>all four marks</u>.
2) Make sure you <u>leave</u> your compass marks <u>showing</u>.
3) You get <u>two equal angles</u>.

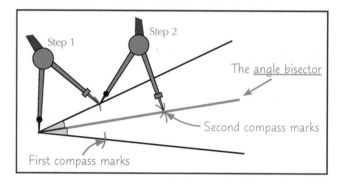

The **Perpendicular** to a **Line** through a **Point**

You'll be given a <u>line</u> and a <u>point</u>, like this...

A ——————— B
•

... or a point that's <u>on</u> the line, like this:

A ———•——— B

> The perpendicular distance from a point to the line is the <u>shortest distance</u> to the line.

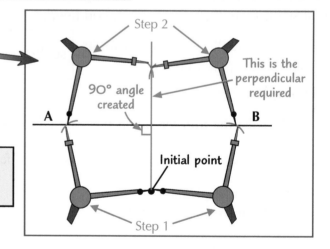

Example

Use an appropriate compass construction and a ruler to show the shortest distance from point P to the line AB.

1) Use the <u>method</u> above:
2) <u>Draw</u> the <u>perpendicular distance</u> from the <u>line</u> to <u>point P</u> with a ruler.

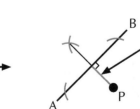

This is the shortest distanc

Practice Question

1) Draw a 70° angle and bisect it. Leave your construction marks showing.

Triangle Construction

How you construct a triangle depends on what information you're given about the triangle...

Sides Only — Use a **Ruler and Compasses**

— **Example** —

Construct the triangle ABC where AB = 5 cm, BC = 3 cm, AC = 4 cm.

1) First, <u>sketch and label</u> a triangle so you know roughly what's needed. It doesn't matter which line you make the base line.

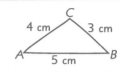

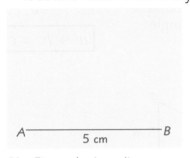

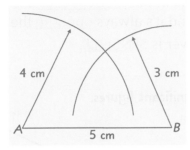

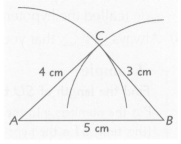

2) Draw the <u>base line</u>. <u>Label</u> the ends A and B.

3) For AC, set the <u>compasses</u> to <u>4 cm</u>, put the point at A and <u>draw an arc</u>. For BC, set the compasses to <u>3 cm</u>, put the point at B and <u>draw an arc</u>.

4) Where the <u>arcs cross</u> is <u>point C</u>. Now you can finish your triangle.

You can use compasses like this to draw sides in any shape. If you know the angle too, see below.

Sides and Angles — Use a **Ruler** and **Protractor**

You could also use a set square to draw a right angle.

— **Example** —

Construct triangle DEF. DE = 6 cm, DEF = 90°, and angle EDF = 40°.

1) <u>Roughly sketch and label</u> the triangle.

2) Draw the <u>base line</u>.

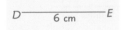

3) Draw <u>angle DEF</u> (the angle at E) — place the centre of the protractor over E, measure <u>90°</u> and put a dot.

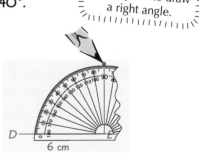

4) Draw a <u>straight line</u> from E going through the dot.

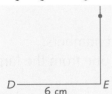

5) Do steps 3 and 4 again, but this time for <u>angle EDF</u>.

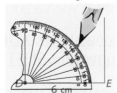

6) <u>Label</u> the point where the two lines meet F.

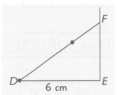

Practice Question

1) Construct a triangle with sides 3 cm, 4 cm and 4 cm. Leave your construction marks showing.

Section 5 — Geometry and Measures

Pythagoras' Theorem

Pythagoras' theorem sounds scary but it's actually OK. There's just one little formula to learn...

Pythagoras' Theorem — $a^2 + b^2 = c^2$

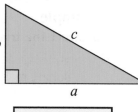

1) PYTHAGORAS' THEOREM only works for RIGHT-ANGLED TRIANGLES.
2) Pythagoras uses two sides to find the third side.
3) The BASIC FORMULA for Pythagoras is $a^2 + b^2 = c^2$.
4) Make sure you get the numbers in the RIGHT PLACE. c is the longest side (called the hypotenuse) and it's always opposite the right angle.
5) Always CHECK that your answer is SENSIBLE.

$$a^2 + b^2 = c^2$$

Example

Find the length of SU to 3 significant figures.

Put the numbers into the formula
(this time, ST is the hypotenuse):

$SU^2 + 5^2 = 11^2$

$SU^2 + 25 = 121$

$\quad SU^2 = 121 - 25 = 96$

$\quad\quad SU = \sqrt{96} = 9.797... = 9.80$ m (to 3 s.f.)

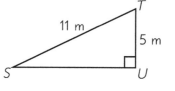

Check the answer is sensible — yes, it's a bit shorter than the longest side.

Example

Find the distance between points S and T to 1 d.p.

1) Work out the coordinates of S and T. $S = (1, 2) \quad T = (6, 5)$

2) Work out the horizontal distance between S and T.   Horizontal $= 6 - 1 = 5$ units

3) Now find the vertical distance between S and T.   Vertical $= 5 - 2 = 3$ units

4) The distance between S and T is the hypotenuse (c) of the triangle. So substitute these values into the equation for Pythagoras' theorem.

$5^2 + 3^2 = c^2$

$34 = c^2$

$c = \sqrt{34}$

$c = 5.8309... = 5.8$ units

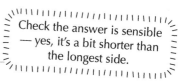

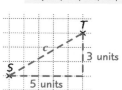

If you're getting a bit confused, here's a quick summary of what you have to do:

1) **SQUARE THEM** — SQUARE THE TWO NUMBERS that you are given, (use the x^2 button if you've got your calculator).

2) **ADD or SUBTRACT** — To find the longest side, ADD the two squared numbers. To find a shorter side, SUBTRACT the smaller one from the larger.

3) **SQUARE ROOT** — Finally, take the SQUARE ROOT (use the $\sqrt{}$ button on your calculator).

Practice Question

1) The two shorter sides of a right-angled triangle are 5 cm and 12 cm long. Find the longest side.

Summary Questions

Congratulations — you've got to the end. Section 5 is a tough one so here's some practice for you.
Try these questions and tick off each one when you get it right.
• When you've done all the questions for a topic and are completely happy with it, tick off the topic.

L1) 2D Shapes (p67-69) ☐

1) Write down the number of lines of symmetry
   and the order of rotational symmetry for a rhombus. ☐
2) Name 2 quadrilaterals that have 2 pairs of equal angles. ☐
3) A regular polygon has 8 sides. What is the name of this polygon? ☐

L1) Perimeter and Area (p70-73) ☐

4) Find the perimeter and area of a rectangle that measures 11 cm by 5 cm. ☐
5) A rectangle has a perimeter of 68 cm.
   If one of its sides is 4 cm long, what is its area? ☐
6) Find the area of the shape on the right. ☐
7) Find the area of a circle with radius 8 cm, to 2 decimal places. ☐
L2) 8) Find the area of a sector with an internal angle of 72° in
   a circle with radius 6 cm to 1 decimal place. ☐

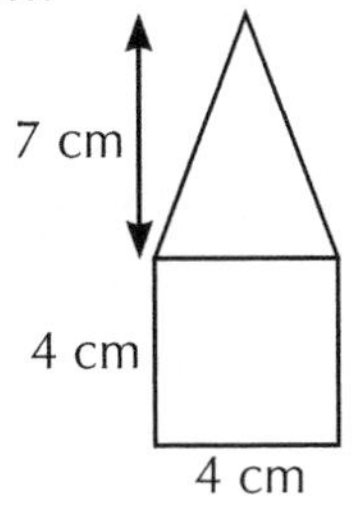

(7 cm, 4 cm, 4 cm labels on diagram)

L1) 3D Shapes (p74-77) ☐

9) Write down the number of faces and edges of a cube. ☐
10) Draw the net of a cuboid measuring 2 cm by 3 cm by 5 cm.
    Find the cuboid's volume and surface area. ☐
L3) 11) Find the volume of a prism with cross-sectional area 6 cm² and length 8 cm. ☐

L1) Angles (p78-82) ☐

12) Give an example of   a) an acute angle,   b) an obtuse angle,   c) a reflex angle. ☐
13) What type of angles do you find in a Z-shape on parallel lines? ☐
14) Find the size of angle x in the diagram on the right. ☐
L2) 15) Work out the size of an exterior angle and an interior angle
    of a regular decagon (a 10-sided shape). ☐
L2) 16) What is the sum of interior angles in a regular octagon? ☐

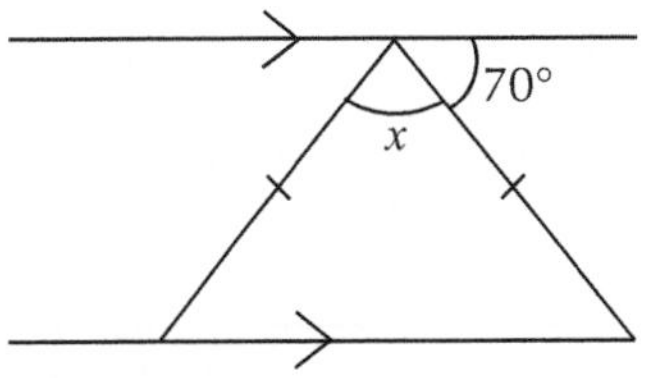

(70°, x labels on triangle diagram)

L1) Transformations and Constructions (p83-87) ☐

17) How many quarter turns are in 360°? How many half turns are in 540°? ☐
18) Point P (3, 4) is reflected in the line $y = 2$. What are the new coordinates of point P? ☐
L2) 19) A triangle has vertices with coordinates (1, 1), (4, 1) and (3, 4). Write the coordinates
    of the vertices of the triangle after an enlargement with scale factor 3 and centre (–1, 0). ☐
20) Construct triangle ABC, where AB = 3 cm, AC = 3.5 cm and angle CAB = 50°. ☐

L3) Pythagoras (p88) ☐

21) Use Pythagoras' theorem to find the length of the missing side to 3 s.f. ☐
22) Find the distance between the coordinates (–1, 2) and (2, 6). ☐

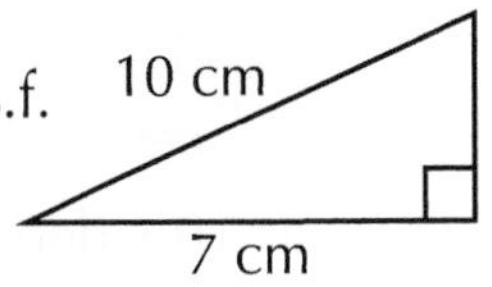

(10 cm, 7 cm labels on triangle diagram)

Probability

Believe me, probability's not as bad as you think it is, but you must learn the basic facts.

All Probabilities are Between 0 and 1

Probabilities can only have values <u>from 0 to 1</u> (including those values).
You can show the probability of any event happening on this <u>scale</u> of 0 to 1

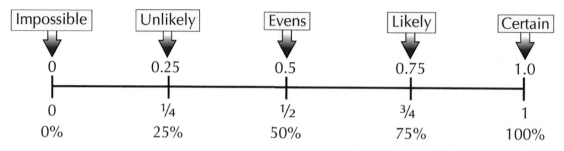

| Impossible | Unlikely | Evens | Likely | Certain |

0	0.25	0.5	0.75	1.0
0	¼	½	¾	1
0%	25%	50%	75%	100%

If All the Outcomes are Equally Likely, Use This Formula

<u>Outcomes</u> are just 'things that could happen'. If you repeat an experiment, you can get <u>different</u> outcomes — think, if you keep rolling a fair dice, you're likely to get different numbers.

Use the formula below to find probabilities for a <u>fair</u> spinner, coin or dice.
A spinner/coin/dice is 'fair' when it's <u>equally likely</u> to land on <u>any</u> of its sides.

$$\text{Probability} = \frac{\text{Number of ways for something to happen}}{\text{Total number of possible outcomes}}$$

This formula works for other cases where all the possible outcomes are <u>equally likely</u> (so in the example below, there's an <u>equal chance</u> of picking any one ball).

┌─ **Example** ─────────────────────────────
A bag contains 6 blue balls, 5 red balls and 9 green balls.
Find the probability of picking out a green ball.

Just put the numbers into the formula above:

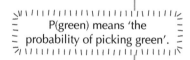
P(green) means 'the probability of picking green'.

$$P(green) = \frac{\text{Number of green balls}}{\text{Total number of balls}} = \frac{9}{20} \text{ (or 0.45)}$$

Probabilities Add Up to 1

1) If <u>only one</u> possible result can happen at a time, then the probabilities of <u>all</u> the results <u>add up to 1</u>

Probabilities always ADD UP to 1

2) So since something must either <u>happen</u> or <u>not happen</u> (i.e. <u>only one</u> of these can happen at a time):

P(event happens) + P(event doesn't happen) = 1

3) In the example above, the probability of <u>not</u> picking green = 1 − P(green) = 1 − 0.45 = 0.55

Practice Question

1) On a fair 10-sided spinner numbered 1-10, what is the probability of spinning:
   a) A 7?   b) An odd number?   c) An even number?

Probability

Probability gets more interesting when more than one thing is happening at the same time.

Use **Tables** to List **All Possible Outcomes**

When there are <u>multiple things</u> happening you can use a <u>table</u> to list all the possible outcomes.

> **Example**
>
> The two fair spinners on the right are each spun once.
>
>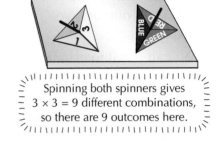
>
> a) Complete this table showing the possible outcomes.
>
> The possible outcomes for one spinner go <u>down the side</u>. The outcomes for the other spinner go <u>along the top</u>.
>
> | | Red | Blue | Green |
> |---|---|---|---|
> | 1 | 1R | 1B | 1G |
> | 2 | 2R | 2B | 2G |
> | 3 | 3R | 3B | 3G |
>
> Spinning both spinners gives $3 \times 3 = 9$ different combinations, so there are 9 outcomes here.
>
> b) Find the probability of spinning a 2 and a green (2G).
>
> $$P(2G) = \frac{\text{ways to spin 2 and green}}{\text{total number of possible outcomes}} = \frac{1}{9}$$
>
> c) Find the probability of spinning an odd number and a red.
>
> 1R and 3R
>
> $$P(\text{odd and red}) = \frac{\text{ways to spin odd and red}}{\text{total number of possible outcomes}} = \frac{2}{9}$$

> **Example**
>
> (L2) A coin is tossed three times.
> Find the probability of getting heads exactly twice.
>
> There are 3 ways to get heads exactly twice: (HHT), (HTH) and (THH), and 8 possible outcomes in total.
>
> | | Possible Outcomes | | | | | | | |
> |---|---|---|---|---|---|---|---|---|
> | Throw 1 | H | H | H | T | H | T | T | T |
> | Throw 2 | H | H | T | H | T | H | T | T |
> | Throw 3 | H | T | H | H | T | T | H | T |
>
> $$P(\text{two heads}) = \frac{\text{ways to throw heads twice}}{\text{total number of possible outcomes}} = \frac{3}{8}$$

Use Probability to Find an "**Expected Frequency**"

1) Once you know the <u>probability</u> of something, you can <u>predict</u> how many times it will happen in a certain number of trials.

2) For example, you can predict the number of heads you could expect if you tossed a fair coin 50 times. This prediction is called the <u>expected frequency</u>.

> Expected frequency = probability × number of trials

> **Example**
>
> The probability of someone winning a game at a fair is 0.12.
> Estimate the number of times you would expect them to win if they played the game 50 times.
>
> Expected number of wins = probability of a win × number of trials
>
> $$= 0.12 \times 50 = 6$$
>
> This is an estimate. They might not win exactly 6 times, but it should be close.

Practice Questions

1) Two fair dice numbered 1-6 are rolled, and their scores added together. By listing all the possible outcomes in a table, find the probability that the total score is greater than 7

2) A spinner has a probability of 0.3 of landing on blue. If the spinner is spun 40 times, estimate how many times you would expect it to land on blue.

Experimental Probability

Dice aren't always fair — you can use experimental probability to decide if they are or aren't.

Fair or Unfair?

'Fair' just means that all the possible scores are equally likely.

1) You can use the formula on p.90 to work out that the probability of rolling a 3 on a dice is $\frac{1}{6}$.
2) BUT this only works if it's a <u>fair dice</u>. If the dice is <u>unfair</u> (<u>biased</u>) then each number <u>won't</u> have an equal chance of being rolled.
3) This is where <u>experimental probability</u> is useful. You can use it to <u>estimate</u> probabilities when things aren't fair.

Do the Experiment Again and Again and Again...

You need to do an experiment <u>over and over again</u> and count how often a result happens (its <u>frequency</u>). Then you can find its <u>experimental probability</u>.

$$\text{Experimental probability} = \frac{\text{Frequency}}{\text{Number of times you tried the experiment}}$$

Sometimes the experimental probability is called the 'relative frequency'.

You can use the <u>experimental probability</u> of a result as an <u>estimate</u> of its <u>probability</u>.

— Example —

A dice was rolled 100 times. The results are in the table below.
Estimate the probability of getting each of the scores.

Score	1	2	3	4	5	6
Frequency	15	13	4	45	16	7

The dice was rolled <u>100 times</u>, so <u>divide</u> each of the frequencies by 100 to find the <u>experimental probabilities</u>.

Score	1	2	3	4	5	6
Experimental Probability	$\frac{15}{100} = 0.15$	$\frac{13}{100} = 0.13$	$\frac{4}{100} = 0.04$	$\frac{45}{100} = 0.45$	$\frac{16}{100} = 0.16$	$\frac{7}{100} = 0.07$

The <u>MORE TIMES</u> you do the experiment, the <u>MORE ACCURATE</u> your estimate of the probability will be. If you rolled the above dice <u>1000 times</u>, you'd get a <u>better</u> estimate of the probabilities.

For a <u>fair</u> dice or spinner, the experimental probabilities should all be <u>roughly the same</u> after a large number of trials. If some of them are very <u>different</u>, the dice or spinner is probably <u>biased</u>.

If it's fair, you'd expect roughly the same number of each score.

— Example —

Do the above results suggest that the dice is biased?

Yes, because on a <u>fair</u> dice, you'd expect all the probabilities to be about the <u>same</u> (you'd expect each probability to be about 1 ÷ 6 = 0.17(ish)). These probabilities are very <u>different</u> (the probability of rolling a 4 is <u>much higher</u> than the probability of rolling a 3), so the dice is <u>biased</u>.

Practice Question

1) A 3-sided spinner is spun 100 times — it lands on red 43 times, blue 24 times and green the other times. Calculate the experimental probability of spinning each colour.

Data and Tables

Data is what statistics is all about. You've got to collect it, process it and then interpret it.

Discrete Data Can Only Take Certain Values

1) If your data is something that's <u>countable</u> in whole numbers or can only take certain <u>individual values</u>, it's called <u>discrete data</u>.

> Data that isn't discrete is called continuous.

2) Things like the <u>number of points</u> scored in a game or the <u>number of people</u> shopping on one day are examples of discrete data.

3) Discrete data can be shown in <u>frequency tables</u> — they show <u>how many</u> things there are in each <u>category</u>.

Vehicle	Frequency
Car	5
Bus	20
Lorry	31

There are 5 cars, 20 buses, etc.

Each tally mark represents 'one'. Tally marks are grouped into fives to make them easier to count.

Name	Laps	Frequency
Zac	ЖЖ ЖЖ IIII	14
Alice	ЖЖ	5
Paul	ЖЖ ЖЖ II	12

Two-Way Tables Show Two Types of Information

<u>Two-way tables</u> are a kind of frequency table — they show you <u>how many</u> things are in each category, but for <u>two sets of categories</u> at once.

Example

Simon asked 40 people in his school how many musical instruments they play.

a) Complete the two-way table to show Simon's results.

	None	1 instrument	2 or more instruments	TOTAL	
Boys	24 − 5 − 8 = 11	8	12 − 7 = 5	24	← Total boys
Girls	7	16 − 7 − 7 = 2	7	40 − 24 = 16	← Total girls
TOTAL	11 + 7 = 18	8 + 2 = 10	12	40	← Total people

↑ Total who don't play an instrument   ↑ Total who play 1 instrument   ↑ Total who play 2 or more instruments

To fill in a two-way table, you need to look at the <u>differences</u> between the '<u>TOTAL</u>' row or column, and the other data you're given. E.g. to start you could:

- Work out the number of boys who play 2 or more instruments. The total number of people who play 2 or more instruments is 12, and 7 of these are girls, so 12 − 7 = 5 boys, OR
- Work out the number of girls Simon asked. The total number of people Simon asked is 40, and 24 of these are boys, so Simon asked 40 − 24 = 16 girls.

b) Simon chooses someone who plays 1 instrument at random.
What is the probability that it is a boy?

1) Find the <u>total</u> number of people who play <u>1 instrument</u>.   10 people play 1 instrument

2) Find the number of these people who are <u>boys</u>.   8 boys play 1 instrument

3) Put the numbers into the <u>probability formula</u> given on page 90, and <u>simplify</u> if possible.   Probability = $\frac{8}{10} = \frac{4}{5}$

Practice Question

1) Look at the purple table in the example above.
Given that a student is a girl, find the probability that she plays 1 instrument.

Sorting Information

Venn diagrams are a way of displaying data in intersecting circles — they're very pretty.

Venn Diagrams Sort Things Into Groups

Venn diagrams sort things into groups, where all the members of a group have a certain property.

> E.g.   All the numbers in a group are even.
> All the people in a group have brown hair.

1) Each group is represented by a circle. The circles can show the actual members of the groups, or just the numbers of members.

2) There is a region where the circles overlap. If something fits into both groups, it goes here.

3) If something doesn't fit into a group, it goes in the rectangle, outside of the circles.

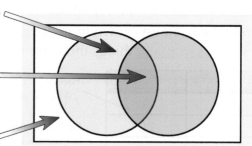

Example

A class of children were asked whether they have any brothers or sisters. This diagram shows how many people gave each answer.

a) **How many children have only a sister?**
This is the number in the part of the 'Sister' circle that doesn't overlap.   12 children

b) **How many children have a brother and a sister?**
Children who have a brother and a sister are recorded in the 'overlap' region.   5 children

c) **How many children have a brother?**
This is everyone in the 'Brother' circle, including the overlap.   9 + 5 = 14 children

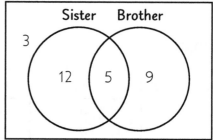

Example

(L3) Sort the following numbers into the Venn diagram below:
5, 9, 11, 1, 8, 40, 12, 7, 16, 21, 24, 2, 3, 4, 44, 10

1) Start by writing out all the numbers that are multiples of 4 and all the numbers that are factors of 80
Multiples of 4 — 8, 40, 12, 16, 24, 4, 44
Factors of 80 — 5, 1, 8, 40, 16, 2, 4, 10

2) The numbers that are in both lists go in the overlap region and the rest go in just 'multiples of 4' or 'factors of 80'
Factors of 80 and multiples of 4 — 8, 40, 16, 4
Multiples of 4 — 12, 24, 44, Factors of 80 — 5, 1, 2, 10

3) The remaining numbers go in the rectangle, outside the circles.
Neither group — 9, 11, 7, 21, 3

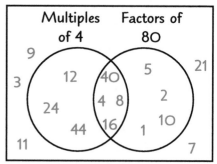

Venn diagrams don't just sort numbers — you can sort shapes, animals, people...

Practice Question

(L3) 1) Sort the following numbers into a copy of the Venn diagram on the right.
9, 2, 15, 14, 11, 33, 25, 7, 12, 24, 30, 100, 73, 42, 6, 31, 28, 3, 47

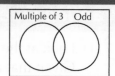

Sorting Information

Carroll diagrams are another way of sorting data visually.

Carroll Diagrams *Group Things Using* '**Yes**' *or* '**No**'

1) <u>Carroll diagrams</u> are a bit like <u>Venn diagrams</u> — they sort things into <u>groups</u>, but in table form.

2) You can sort different bits of data in a data set, according to whether they have a <u>certain property or not</u>. E.g. Is it less than 20 or not? Is it a factor of 60 or not? Can it fly or not?

Example

Sort the following list of numbers into the Carroll diagram below.
8, 4, 12, 6, 1, 7, 18, 36, 73, 60, 44, 54

Multiple of 6	Not a multiple of 6

18   12
  6   54
60   36
	8
	  1 44
	4 7 73

This Carroll diagram sorts numbers depending on whether they're a <u>multiple of 6</u>.

Go through the numbers, working out whether each one is a <u>multiple of 6 or not</u>. Write each number in the correct box.

Cross each number off as you go to keep track of which ones you've sorted.

Sorting By **Two Properties**

Carroll diagrams are often used to sort things depending on <u>two</u> properties.

E.g.   Is it less than 7 or not <u>AND</u> is it an even number or not?
Does it have feathers or not <u>AND</u> can it fly or not?

Example

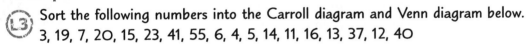

Sort the following numbers into the Carroll diagram and Venn diagram below.
3, 19, 7, 20, 15, 23, 41, 55, 6, 4, 5, 14, 11, 16, 13, 37, 12, 40

Both diagrams sort numbers depending on whether they're a <u>prime number</u> or not, <u>AND</u> whether they're <u>less than 15</u> or not.

1) For each number, first work out if it's a <u>prime number or not</u>.

2) Then work out if it's <u>less than 15 or not</u>.

3) Write each number in the <u>correct part</u> of each diagram.

	Prime number	Not a prime number

Less than 15	3 7 13
	  11 5
		6 4
		  14 12

Not less than 15	37 23 19 41	20 15 55 16 40

Carroll and Venn diagrams are just different ways of displaying the data — they both tell you the same information.

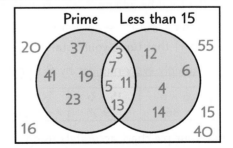

Practice Question

1) Draw a Carroll diagram to sort all the numbers from 0 to 15, depending on whether they're multiples of 5 or not, and whether they're factors of 20 or not.

Graphs and Charts

There are lots of diagrams for displaying data — let's start off with pictograms and pie charts.

Pictograms Use Pictures Instead of Numbers

Every pictogram has a <u>key</u> telling you what one symbol represents.

> With pictograms, you <u>MUST</u> use the <u>KEY</u>.

--- Example ---

This pictogram shows how many pizzas were sold by a pizzeria on different days.

a) How many pizzas were sold on Tuesday?

There's <u>1 whole circle</u> (= 20 pizzas)...   20 + 10
...plus <u>half</u> a circle (= 10 pizzas).   = 30 pizzas

<u>Key:</u> ◯ represents 20 pizzas

Monday	◯◯
Tuesday	◯◖
Wednesday	◯◯
Thursday	◯◯◔
Friday	●●●◖

b) 70 pizzas were sold on Friday.
Use this information to complete the diagram.
You need <u>3 whole circles</u> (= 60 pizzas),
<u>plus</u> another <u>half a circle</u> (= 10 pizzas).

Reading Pie Charts

Learn the <u>Golden Rule</u> for Pie Charts: The TOTAL of Everything = 360°

--- Example ---

Some geography students were asked to name their favourite volcano. The results are displayed in the pie chart. What fraction of the students chose Etna?

Just remember that 'everything = 360°'.

Fraction that chose Etna = $\dfrac{\text{angle of Etna}}{\text{angle of everything}} = \dfrac{60°}{360°} = \dfrac{1}{6}$

To find the size of a sector as a percentage of the full pie chart, divide the angle by 360, then multiply by 100.

Drawing Pie Charts

--- Example ---

Draw a pie chart to show the information about the types of sandwiches served in a cafe.

Sandwich	Cheese	Ham	Chicken	Tuna	Egg
Number	6	15	20	16	3

1. Find the <u>total</u> by <u>adding</u>.   6 + 15 + 20 + 16 + 3 = 60

2. 'Everything = 360°' — so find the <u>multiplier</u>
(or <u>divider</u>) that turns your total into 360°.   Multiplier = 360 ÷ 60 = 6

3. Now <u>multiply every number</u> by 6 to get the <u>angle</u> for each sector.

Angle	6 × 6 = 36°	15 × 6 = 90°	20 × 6 = 120°	16 × 6 = 96°	3 × 6 = 18°	Total = 360°

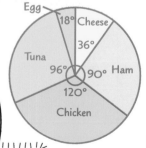

4. Draw your pie chart accurately using a <u>protractor</u>.

Here, 6° represents one sandwich.

Practice Question

1) In the volcano example above, 48 students were asked in total. How many chose Vesuvius?

Graphs and Charts

Another page on graphs and charts — this time, it's line graphs and bar charts.

Line Graphs

1) A <u>line graph</u> is a set of points joined with straight lines.

2) They often have '<u>time</u>' along the bottom to show how something <u>changes</u> over time.

3) This graph <u>peaks</u> in <u>2011</u>, which shows that this is the year with the <u>highest sales</u>.

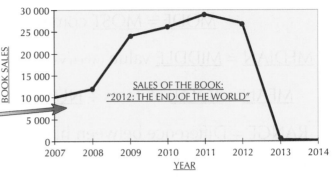

4) You can draw <u>two line graphs</u> on the same grid to <u>compare</u> two things.

5) These graphs show clearly that as the year went on, <u>fewer</u> people wore <u>earmuffs</u> and <u>more</u> people wore <u>sunglasses</u>.

Conversion graphs are another type of line graph (see page 48).

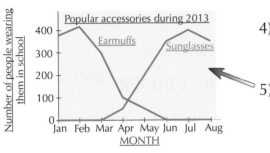

Bar Charts

1) On a bar chart, the numbers of things are shown by the heights of the different bars.

2) Bar-line graphs are just like bar charts but with thin lines instead of bars.

3) Dual bar charts show two sets of data on one chart, by using two bars for each category.

4) Frequency diagrams are bar charts that show data from a frequency table (see page 100).

— **Example** —

Draw a bar chart to show the data in the table below.

	Right-handed	Left-handed	Ambidextrous
Frequency	7	3	2

1) Label both of the axes.
2) Draw a bar for each of the three categories.

Bars representing different categories are separated by gaps.

— **Example** —

Draw a bar chart to show the data in the table below.

	Right-handed	Left-handed	Ambidextrous
Boys	3	2	1
Girls	4	1	1

Split each category into separate bars to show girls and boys.

You'll need a key like this.

Practice Question

1) 32 pupils at a school are asked which sports team they are in. Their results are shown in the table on the right.

Use the data to draw a bar chart.

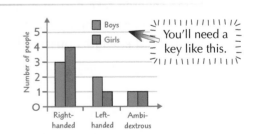

Team	Frequency
A	4
B	7
C	11
D	2
E	8

Section 6 — Probability and Statistics

Mean, Median, Mode and Range

Mean, median, mode and range pop up all the time — make sure you know what they are.

MODE = MOST common

MEDIAN = MIDDLE value (when values are in order of size)

MEAN = TOTAL of items ÷ NUMBER of items

RANGE = Difference between highest and lowest

REMEMBER:
Mode = most (emphasise the 'mo'
in each when you say them)
Median = mid (emphasise the
m*d in each when you say them)
Mean is just the average, but it's
mean 'cos you have to work it out

The *Golden* Rule

There's one vital step for finding the median that lots of people forget:

Always REARRANGE the data in ASCENDING ORDER (and check you have the same number of entries!)

You must do this when finding the median, but it's also really useful for working out the mode.

Example

Find the median, mode, mean and range of these numbers: 6, 4, 7, 1, 2, 6, 3, 5

The **MEDIAN** is the middle value (when they're arranged in order of size) — so first, rearrange the numbers.

Check you have the same number of values after you've rearranged them.

When there are two middle numbers, the median is halfway between the two.

1, 2, 3, (4, 5) 6, 6, 7

← 4 numbers this side ↑ 4 numbers this side →
Median = 4.5

MODE (or modal value) is the most common value. Mode = 6

$$\text{MEAN} = \frac{\text{total of items}}{\text{number of items}} \qquad \frac{1+2+3+4+5+6+6+7}{8} = \frac{34}{8} = 4.25$$

RANGE = difference between highest and lowest values, i.e. between 7 and 1 $7 - 1 = 6$

You might be asked to compare two data sets using the mean, median or mode and the range.

Example

Some children take part in a 'guess the length of the snake' competition.
Here is some information about the lengths they guess.
Compare the lengths guessed by the boys and the girls.

Boys: Mean = 1.2 m, Range = 0.2 m
Girls: Mean = 2.1 m, Range = 1.4 m

1) Compare the means: The girls' mean is higher than the boys' mean, so the girls generally guessed longer lengths.

2) Compare the ranges: The girls' guesses have a bigger range, so the lengths guessed by the girls are more spread out.

Two final facts to finish: 1) Some data sets have more than one mode, or no mode at all.
2) Some measurements may be unusual, e.g. values much higher or lower than the rest. These are called outliers.

Practice Question

1) Find the median, mode, mean and range of these numbers: 10, 12, 8, 15, 9, 12, 11

Averages from Frequency Tables

You've seen how to do it with a list of numbers — now to finding averages from frequency tables.

Find *Averages* from *Frequency Tables*

You can easily find <u>averages</u> and the <u>range</u> from frequency tables...

1) The <u>MODE</u> is just the <u>CATEGORY with the MOST ENTRIES</u> (i.e. the highest frequency).

2) The <u>RANGE</u> is found from the <u>extremes of the first column</u>.

3) The <u>MEDIAN</u> is the <u>CATEGORY</u> of the <u>middle value</u>.

4) To find the <u>MEAN</u>, you use TOTAL of items ÷ NUMBER of items. The number of items is the 2nd column total. You can find the <u>TOTAL</u> of the items by adding a 3rd column.

Categories → How many →

Number of cats	Frequency	
0	15	
1	22	
2	16	
3	7	

Mysterious 3rd column...

Here the <u>3rd column</u> would contain the values of '<u>Number of cats × frequency</u>'.

Example

Some people were asked how many posters they have on their bedroom walls. The table shows the results. Find the mode, range, mean and median of the data.

Number of posters	Frequency
0	1
1	10
2	12
3	9
4	6
5	2

(1) The <u>MODE</u> is the <u>category</u> with the <u>highest frequency</u>.

The highest frequency is 12 for '2 posters', so <u>MODE</u> = 2

(2) The <u>RANGE</u> is the <u>difference</u> between the highest and lowest numbers of posters — that's 5 posters and no posters, so:

<u>RANGE</u> = 5 − 0 = 5

(3) To find the <u>MEAN</u>, <u>add a 3rd column</u> to the table showing '<u>number of posters × frequency</u>'. <u>Add up</u> these values to find the <u>total number of posters</u> of all the people asked.

Number of posters	Frequency	No. of posters × Frequency
0	1	0
1	10	10
2	12	24
3	9	27
4	6	24
5	2	10
Total	40	95

<u>MEAN</u> = $\dfrac{\text{3rd column total}}{\text{2nd column total}}$ = $\dfrac{95}{40}$ = 2.375

total number of posters
total number of people asked

Total number of people asked.   Total number of posters owned.

(4) The <u>MEDIAN</u> is the <u>category</u> of the <u>middle</u> value. Work out its <u>position</u>, then <u>count through</u> the 2nd column to find it.

There are 40 values, so the middle value is halfway between the 20th and 21st values. There are a total of (1 + 10) = 11 values in the first two categories, and another 12 in the third category takes you to 23 in total. So the 20th and 21st values must both be in the category '2 posters', which means the <u>MEDIAN</u> is 2

Practice Question

1) Find the mode, range, mean and median for the cats frequency table at the top of the page.

Averages from Frequency Diagrams

That's frequency tables out of the way — now how to find averages from frequency diagrams.

Find **Averages** from **Frequency Diagrams**

1) The <u>MODE</u> is the category with the <u>TALLEST BAR</u> (i.e. the highest frequency).

2) The <u>RANGE</u> is found from the <u>extremes of the values</u> <u>on the horizontal axis</u>.

3) The <u>MEDIAN</u> is the <u>CATEGORY</u> which contains the <u>middle value</u>.

4) To find the <u>MEAN</u>, you use | TOTAL of items ÷ NUMBER of items.

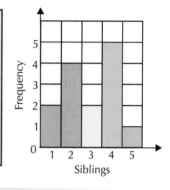

Example

The graph shows how many cakes the contestants in a cake eating competition managed to eat.

a) Find the mode of the data.

> The <u>MODE</u> is the <u>category</u> with the <u>highest frequency.</u>

The highest frequency is 7 for '5 cakes', so mode = 5

b) Find: i) the total number of cakes eaten
   ii) the total number of contestants
   iii) the mean number of cakes eaten

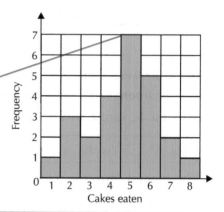

(1) To find the <u>total number of cakes eaten</u>, you need to multiply the <u>frequency</u> (or height) for each bar by its <u>category value</u> — this gives the number of cakes represented by the bar. <u>Add up</u> these values to find the <u>total number of cakes</u> eaten by the contestants.

<u>TOTAL CAKES</u> = (1 × 1) + (2 × 3) + (3 × 2) + (4 × 4) +
       (5 × 7) + (6 × 5) + (7 × 2) + (8 × 1) = 116

(2) To find the <u>total number of contestants</u>, just <u>add up</u> the <u>frequencies</u>, (the heights) of all the bars.

<u>TOTAL CONTESTANTS</u> =
1 + 3 + 2 + 4 + 7 + 5 + 2 + 1 = 25

(3) To find the <u>MEAN</u>, <u>divide</u> the <u>total number of cakes eaten</u> by the <u>total number of contestants</u>.

$$\text{MEAN} = \frac{\text{total number of cakes eaten}}{\text{total number of contestants}} = \frac{116}{25} = 4.64$$

c) Find the median of the data.

> The <u>MEDIAN</u> is the <u>category</u> of the <u>middle</u> value. Work out its position, then <u>count through</u> the bars to find it.

There are 25 values, so the middle value is the 13th. There are a total of (1 + 3 + 2 + 4) = 10 values in the first four categories, and another 7 in the fifth category takes you to 17 in total. So the 13th value must be in the category '5 cakes', which means the median is 5

Practice Question

1) Find the mode, range, mean and median for the frequency diagram at the top of the page.

Scatter Graphs

Scatter graphs are really useful — they show you if there's a link between two things.

Scatter Graphs Show *Correlation*

1) A <u>scatter graph</u> shows how closely two things are <u>related</u>.
   The fancy word for this is <u>CORRELATION</u>.

2) If the two things <u>are related</u>, then you should be able to draw a <u>straight line</u>
   passing <u>pretty close</u> to <u>most</u> of the points on the scatter diagram.

<u>STRONG</u> correlation is when your points make a <u>fairly straight line</u>.

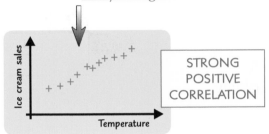

STRONG POSITIVE CORRELATION

If the points form a line sloping <u>uphill</u> from left to right, then there is <u>POSITIVE</u> correlation — both things increase or decrease <u>together</u>.

<u>WEAK</u> correlation means your points <u>don't line up</u> quite so nicely (but you can still draw a line through them).

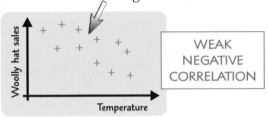

WEAK NEGATIVE CORRELATION

If the points form a line sloping <u>downhill</u> from left to right, then there is <u>NEGATIVE</u> correlation — as one quantity <u>increases</u>, the other <u>decreases</u>.

3) If the two things are <u>not related</u>, you get a load of <u>messy points</u>. This scatter graph is a messy scatter — so there's <u>no correlation</u> between the two things.

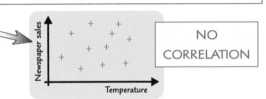

NO CORRELATION

Drawing *Lines of Best Fit*

A <u>line of best fit</u> is a straight line drawn through the middle of a set of data points.
You can use a line of best fit to <u>predict</u> other values.

Example

This graph shows the value of a car (in £'000s) plotted against its age in years.

a) **Describe the strength and type of correlation shown by the graph.**
   The age of car and its value are strongly negatively correlated.

b) **Identify and circle the outlier on the graph.**
   The point at (5, 7.5) doesn't look like it belongs with the rest of the data, so it is an outlier.

c) **Estimate the value of a 3 year old car.**
   1) Draw a <u>line of best fit</u> (shown in <u>blue</u>).
   2) Draw a line <u>up from 3 years</u> to your line, and then <u>across to the other axis</u>.

   So a 3 year old car will be worth about £4500

An outlier can be ignored when drawing a line of best fit

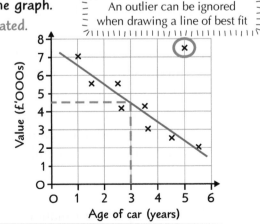

Practice Question

1) Use the graph in the example above to predict the age of a car worth £3500.

Summary Questions

You know what's coming by now — here are some questions to check it's all sunk in.
- Try these questions and <u>tick off each one</u> when you <u>get it right</u>.
- When you've done <u>all the questions</u> for a topic and are <u>completely happy</u> with it, tick off the topic

(L1) <u>Probability (p90-92)</u> ☐

1) What does a probability of 1 mean?

2) In a bag of sweets, there are 5 cola bottles, 2 jelly snakes, 3 chocolate buttons and 2 chocolate mice. Find the probability of randomly picking a cola bottle.

3) In a game, you can either win or lose. If P(win) = 0.1, what is P(lose)?

4) I have a spinner that is half black and half white. I spin it twice. Fill in the table on the right to show all the possible results.

| | | Second spin | |
		Black	White
First spin	Black		BW
	White		

5) I roll a fair dice 60 times. Estimate the number of times it will land on a 5

6) Write down the formula for experimental probability.

(L1) <u>Recording and Sorting Data (p93-95)</u> ☐

7) What is discrete data?

8) This frequency table shows the number of pieces of fruit people eat each day. How many people eat 3 pieces of fruit?

Pieces of Fruit	0	1	2	3	4
Frequency	8	20	17	9	3

9) Write the letter of each shape in the correct place in this Carroll diagram. Ⓐ Ⓑ Ⓒ Ⓓ Ⓔ Ⓕ

	3 sides	Not 3 sides
All straight sides		
Not all straight sides		

(L3) 10) Sort these numbers into a Venn diagram, using the groups 'prime numbers' and 'factors of 8': 1, 2, 3, 4, 5, 6, 7, 8, 9, 10, 11, 12

(L1) <u>Graphs and Charts (p96-97)</u> ☐

11) What do the heights of the bars in a bar chart show?

12) On a pie chart, the angle representing 'not even for £1000' is 30°. If 120 people took part in the survey, how many gave this answer?

13) Draw a bar chart to show the data in the table on the right.

No. of holidays	Frequency
0	5
1	10
2	8
3	3

(L1) <u>Averages and Frequency Tables (p98-100)</u> ☐

14) Find the mode, median, mean and range of this data: 2, 8, 7, 5, 11, 5, 4

15) Using the frequency table opposite, find the mode, median, mean and range for the number of TVs.

Number of TVs	0	1	2	3	4
Frequency	2	10	15	12	1

16) The bar chart on the right shows the number of lengths swum by a group of children in a swimming gala. Find the mode, the total number of lengths swum, the total number of children at the gala and the mean for this data.

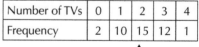

(L1) <u>Scatter Graphs (p101)</u> ☐

17) What type of correlation is shown on the scatter graph on the right?

18) By drawing a line of best fit on the scatter graph, estimate the age of a person who spends 1.5 hours on the Internet per week.

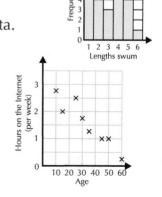

Section 6 — Probability and Statistics

Glossary

We've gathered up some of the most important words you need to know here, so you can remind yourself what they're all about. Words in the definitions that are <u>underlined</u> have their own entry.

2D Shape
A shape with only two dimensions, e.g. width and height.

3D Shape
A solid shape with length, width and height.

Acute Angle
An angle less than 90°.

Addition
Finding the <u>sum</u> when two or more numbers are combined.

Allied Angles
Angles within a pair of <u>parallel lines</u> that add up to 180°.

Alternate Angles
Equal angles within a pair of <u>parallel lines</u>.

Approximation
A number that is not exact because it has been <u>rounded</u> or <u>estimated</u>.

Arc
Part of the <u>circumference</u> of a circle.

Area
The space inside a <u>2D shape</u>.

Arithmetic Sequence
A number <u>sequence</u> where the terms increase or decrease by the same amount each time.

Axis
The <u>vertical</u> and <u>horizontal</u> lines on a graph that the <u>coordinates</u> are measured along. The plural is 'axes'.

Bar Chart
A chart where the heights of the bars show the <u>frequency</u> of each category.

Bearing
The direction of one point from another, measured clockwise from north and given as three figures.

Biased
Where something, e.g. a dice or a spinner, is unfair and more likely to land on one or more of its sides than others.

BODMAS
A way of describing the order that <u>operations</u> should be done in a calculation containing multiple operations.

Brackets
Symbols, such as (), used to group things together.

Cancelling Down
<u>Dividing</u> all the parts of a <u>fraction</u> or <u>ratio</u> by the same number to reduce it to a simpler form.

Carroll Diagram
A table which sorts <u>data</u> depending on whether it has a certain property or not.

Century
100 years.

Certain
Will definitely happen.

Chord
A line drawn across the inside of a circle.

Circumference
The distance around the outside of a circle (its <u>perimeter</u>).

Common Denominator
<u>Fractions</u> have a common <u>denominator</u> when their denominators are the same.

Common Factor
A number that <u>divides</u> exactly into two or more different numbers.

Common Multiple
A number that will <u>divide</u> by two or more different numbers.

Compass (construction)
A tool used for drawing <u>arcs</u> to construct and bisect <u>2D shapes</u>.

Compass (direction)
An instrument that shows the direction of north and the other 7 compass directions.

Congruent
The same shape and size.

Coordinates
A pair of numbers (x, y) that describe the position of a point on a grid or set of <u>axes</u>, e.g. (2, 3).

Correlation
The relationship between two things, usually shown by the points on a <u>scatter graph</u>. Correlation can be either <u>positive</u> or <u>negative</u>.

Corresponding Angles
Equal angles around a pair of <u>parallel lines</u>.

Cross-section
The <u>2D shape</u> you get when you cut a <u>3D shape</u>.

Cube (number)
The result of <u>multiplying</u> a number or letter by itself, then by itself again.

Cube Root
The <u>inverse</u> of <u>cubing</u> a number.

Cube (shape)
A <u>3D shape</u> with 6 identical square <u>faces</u>.

Cuboid
A <u>3D shape</u> with 3 pairs of matching rectangular <u>faces</u>.

Cylinder
A <u>3D shape</u> with a circular <u>cross-section</u> that is the same all the way through.

Data
Pieces of information.

Decade
10 years.

Decimal
A number where tenths, hundredths and thousandths, etc. are written after a decimal point.

Decimal Place
The position of a <u>digit</u> to the right of the decimal point.

Denominator
The bottom number of a <u>fraction</u>.

Diameter
The length across a circle, going through the centre.

Digit

A number from 0 to 9.

Direct Proportion

When the ratio between two things stays the same. If you increase one thing, the other increases at the same rate.

Discrete Data

Data that is countable.

Distance

How far an object has travelled.

Division

The act of sharing a number into equal parts.

Divisor

The number that divides another number.

Edge

Part of a 3D shape, where two faces meet.

Enlargement

Changing an object's size but keeping the shape the same.

Equation

An expression that contains an equals sign. E.g. $y = 2x + 3$.

Equilateral Triangle

A regular triangle, with three equal sides and three equal angles of 60°.

Estimate

An approximate value of a number, often the result of a calculation where rounded numbers have been used instead of the actual values.

Expected Frequency

How many times you'd expect an event to happen during a certain number of trials.

Experimental Probability

An estimate of how likely something is to happen based on the results of an experiment.

Expression

A collection of terms made up of numbers and letters, separated by + or − signs, that doesn't contain an equals sign.

Exterior Angle

The angle between a side of a polygon, and the line extended from a neighbouring side.

Face

A surface of a 3D shape.

Factor

A number that divides exactly into another number.

Factorise

Rewrite an expression by putting in brackets with a factor on the outside.

Fair

Where something, e.g. a dice or a spinner, is equally likely to land on any of its sides.

Formula

A rule written using algebra which can be used to work out a value.

Fraction

A part of a whole, written as one number on top of another.

Frequency

How many items are in a category.

Frequency Diagram

A bar chart that shows data from a frequency table.

Frequency Table

A table showing how many times each value in a set of data occurs.

Geometric Sequence

A number sequence where each term is found by multiplying or dividing the previous term by the same number.

Gradient

The steepness of a line — a measure of how much it slopes.

Highest Common Factor (HCF)

The highest number that can be divided exactly into a set of numbers.

Horizontal

A flat line that runs from left to right.

Hypotenuse

The longest side of a right-angled triangle.

Imperial Units

A non-metric set of units for measuring, including inches, feet, yards, ounces, pounds, stones, pints and gallons.

Impossible

Has no chance of happening.

Improper Fraction

A fraction where the numerator is greater than the denominator.

Inequality

A way of comparing the values of numbers. < means less than, > means greater than, ≤ means less than or equal to and ≥ means greater than or equal to.

Integer

A whole number, positive or negative (including zero).

Interior Angle

An angle within a polygon.

Inverse Operation

The opposite operation. E.g. subtraction is the inverse of addition.

Isosceles Triangle

A triangle with two equal sides and two equal angles.

Kite

A quadrilateral with two pairs of equal sides and one pair of equal angles.

Line Graph

A graph showing two things plotted against each other. The plotted points are joined with straight lines.

Line of Best Fit

A line drawn on a scatter graph which goes through the middle of the set of data points, passing as close to as many of the points as possible.

Line Symmetry

A shape has line symmetry if you can draw on a mirror line where one side of the shape is the exact reflection of the other.

Lowest Common Multiple (LCM)

The smallest number that's in the times tables of a group of numbers.

Map

An accurate drawing showing large distances on a smaller scale.

Mean

The average of a set of data, found by adding up all of the values and dividing by the number of values.

Median

The middle value when you put a set of data in size order.

Metric Units

A standard set of units for measuring, including mm, cm, m, km, g, kg, tonnes, ml and litres.

Millennium

1000 years.

Mirror Line

The line that a shape or object is reflected in.

Mixed Number

A number made up of a whole number part and a fraction part.

Mode

The most common value in a set of data.

Multiple

A value in a number's times table.

Multiplication

The act of multiplying numbers together.

Negative

Any number less than zero.

Negative Correlation

As one thing on a scatter graph increases, the other decreases.

Net

A hollow 3D shape folded out flat.

No Correlation

The points plotted on a scatter graph are spread out and show no relation.

Numerator

The top number of a fraction.

Obtuse Angle

An angle greater than 90° but less than 180°.

Operation

Something you do to one or more numbers, such as add, subtract, multiply or divide.

Order of Rotational Symmetry

The number of positions, in one full turn, you can rotate a shape into so that it looks the same.

Origin

The point with coordinates (0, 0) on a graph. It's where the axes cross.

Outcome

A possible result of a probability trial.

Parabola

The shape a quadratic graph has — it is a symmetrical bucket shape.

Parallel Lines

Lines that are always the same distance apart and never meet.

Parallelogram

A quadrilateral with two pairs of equal parallel sides and two pairs of equal angles.

Percentage

'Per cent' means 'out of 100'. Percentage shows an amount as a number out of 100.

Percentage Change

The amount a value increases or decreases by, given as a percentage of the original value.

Perimeter

The total distance around the outside of a shape.

Perpendicular Lines

Two lines which cross at right angles.

Pi

The number 3.14159265..., written using the Greek letter π.

Pictogram

A chart that displays numbers of things using pictures.

Pie Chart

A chart where the angles of each sector are proportional to the frequency of each category.

Polygon

An enclosed 2D shape whose sides are all straight.

Positive

Any number greater than zero.

Positive Correlation

As one thing on a scatter graph increases, so does the other.

Power

A way of showing that a number or letter is being multiplied by itself a certain number of times. The power tells you how many of the number or letter to multiply together.

Prime Factor

A factor of a number that is a prime number.

Prime Number

A number that has no factors except itself and 1.

Prism

A 3D shape which is the same shape all the way through.

Probability

How likely it is that something will happen.

Product

The result when two things are multiplied together.

Proportion

A part of a whole. Proportions can be written as fractions, decimals or percentages.

Protractor

A tool used for drawing and measuring angles.

Pythagoras' Theorem

A formula linking the lengths of the sides of a right-angled triangle. Pythagoras' theorem states that $a^2 + b^2 = c^2$, where c is the hypotenuse and a and b are the shorter sides.

Quadrant

A quarter of a graph split by the x- and y-axes.

Quadratic

An equation or expression which contains an x^2 term, but no higher powers of x.

Quadrilateral

A four-sided polygon.

Radius

The distance from the centre to the edge of a circle.

Range

The difference between the highest value and the lowest value in a set of data.

Ratio

The amount of one thing compared to another, written e.g. 2 : 1.

Reciprocal

The reciprocal of a number is 1 divided by it. For a fraction, the reciprocal is found by swapping the numerator and the denominator.

Rectangle

A quadrilateral with two pairs of equal sides and four right angles (90°).

Reflection

A transformation where a shape is flipped in a mirror line. OR a mirror image of another shape, with every point the same distance from the mirror line as in the original shape.

Reflex Angle

An angle greater than 180° but less than 360°.

Regular Polygon

A polygon with sides of equal length and angles that are all equal.

Rhombus

A <u>quadrilateral</u> with four equal sides (opposite sides are <u>parallel</u>) and two pairs of equal angles.

Right Angle

An angle of 90°.

Right-Angled Triangle

A <u>triangle</u> with one angle of 90°.

Rotation

Turning an object, either clockwise or anticlockwise, through a given angle around a given point.

Rotational Symmetry

A shape has rotational symmetry if you can <u>rotate</u> it so that it looks exactly the same from a different position.

Rounding

<u>Approximating</u> a number (e.g. writing it with fewer <u>decimal places</u> or as a <u>multiple</u> of 10, 100, etc.)

Scale

The numbers on a <u>map</u> or plan that show how actual distances will be represented on the map.

Scale Drawing

A drawing that is drawn accurately to scale.

Scale Factor

The amount each length increases by in an <u>enlargement</u>.

Scale (measuring)

The number line on a measuring device, which you read to measure something.

Scalene Triangle

A <u>triangle</u> with all three sides and angles different.

Scatter Graph

A graph showing two things plotted against each other. The plotted points are never joined with a line, but the graph may show a <u>line of best fit</u>.

Sector

A wedge-shaped <u>area</u> of a circle.

Segment

The <u>area</u> of a circle when you cut along a <u>chord</u>.

Sequence

A pattern of numbers or shapes that follow a certain rule.

Significant Figures

The first significant figure is the first non-zero <u>digit</u> of a number. Each number that follows after is an additional significant figure.

Similar

When two objects have the same shape but different sizes.

Simplify

Make something simpler, e.g. by <u>dividing</u> by <u>common factors</u> or collecting like <u>terms</u>.

Simultaneous Equations

Two <u>equations</u> with two unknowns that can be solved at the same time.

Solve

To find the value(s) of the unknown(s) that make <u>equations</u> or <u>inequalities</u> true.

Speed

How fast an object is travelling.

Sphere

A perfectly round <u>3D shape</u>.

Square-Based Pyramid

A <u>3D shape</u> made of a square base, and 4 triangular <u>faces</u> that meet at a point.

Square (number)

The result of <u>multiplying</u> a number or letter by itself.

Square Root

The <u>inverse</u> of <u>squaring</u> a number.

Square (shape)

A <u>regular</u> <u>quadrilateral</u>, with four equal sides and four <u>right angles</u> (90°).

Standard Form

A way of writing very small or very large numbers in the form $A \times 10^n$.

Substitute

To replace something in a <u>term</u> with something else, e.g. a letter with a number.

Subtraction

Finding the difference between two numbers.

Sum

The total of some numbers.

Surface Area

The total <u>area</u> of all the <u>faces</u> of a <u>3D shape</u> added together.

Symmetry

A shape has symmetry if it can be <u>reflected</u> or <u>rotated</u> to give the same shape.

Tangent

A straight line that just touches the outside of a circle.

Term (of an expression)

A number, a letter or collection of numbers or letters <u>multiplied</u>/<u>divided</u> together.

Tetrahedron

A <u>3D shape</u> with 4 triangular <u>faces</u> (also known as a triangle-based pyramid).

Time

How long something takes.

Transformation

Changing the size, orientation or position of an object.

Translation

Changing the position of an object by sliding it <u>horizontally</u> and <u>vertically</u>.

Trapezium

A <u>quadrilateral</u> with one pair of <u>parallel</u> sides.

Trial and Improvement

A method of finding a solution or <u>approximate</u> solution to an <u>equation</u> by trying different values that are closer and closer to the correct solution.

Triangle

A three-sided shape.

Triangular Prism

A <u>prism</u> with a triangular <u>cross-section</u>.

Variable

An unknown quantity, often represented by a letter.

Venn Diagram

A diagram that sorts things into different groups, using circles to represent the groups.

Vertex

The corner of a <u>2D</u> or <u>3D shape</u>.

Vertical

A line going straight up and down.

Volume

The amount of space that a <u>3D shape</u> occupies.

x-axis

The <u>horizontal</u> <u>axis</u> of a graph.

y-axis

The <u>vertical</u> <u>axis</u> of a graph.

Answers

Section 1 — Numbers

Page 3 — Calculating Tips
1) a) 1   b) 14   c) 14
2) a) 21   b) 2   c) 4

Page 4 — Calculating Tips
1) 10

Page 5 — Calculating Tips
1) a) 50   Check: 50 − 16 = 34
                  or 50 − 34 = 16
   b) 49   Check: 49 + 59 = 108
                  or 59 + 49 = 108
   c) 161   Check: 161 ÷ 7 = 23
                  or 161 ÷ 23 = 7
   d) 26   Check: 26 × 6 = 156
                     6 × 26 = 156
2) a) 5   b) 5

Page 6 — Place Value
1) a) Nine million, nine hundred and five thousand, two hundred and eighty-five.
   b) Six million, fifty-four thousand, two hundred and three.
2) a) six tenths
   b) seven thousandths

Page 7 — Ordering Numbers
1) 318, 107, 35, −5, −6, −16, −24, −115
2) a) 30 000 > 29 950
   b) 0.005 < 0.045

Page 8 — Addition and Subtraction
1) a) 797   b) 852   c) 18.45
2) 12.35 seconds

Page 9 — Multiplying by 10, 100, etc.
1) a) 64   b) 85 200   c) 88.5
   d) 270   e) 1920
2) 3200

Page 10 — Dividing by 10, 100, etc.
1) a) 0.859   b) 356.98
   c) 0.06752   d) 104
2) £67.98

Page 11 — Multiplying Without a Calculator
1) a) 3776   b) 1554   c) 32 576

Page 12 — Dividing Without a Calculator
1) a) 16   b) 22   c) 12.5
2) 6 gummy worms

Page 13 — Multiplying and Dividing with Decimals
1) a) 120.54   b) 2.598   c) 1.02
2) 64   3) 640

Page 14 — Negative Numbers
1) a) 5   b) −15   c) 18   d) −3
2) 14.1 °C

Page 15 — Prime Numbers
1) 73, 83

Page 16 — Multiples, Factors and Prime Factors
1) a) 15, 30, 45, 60, 75, 90, 105, 120
   b) 1, 2, 4, 8, 16, 32, 64
2) 60, 72
3) a) $2 \times 2 \times 3 \times 5 \times 5$
   b) $2^2 \times 3 \times 5^2$

Page 17 — LCM and HCF
1) 36   2) 16

Page 18 — Fractions, Decimals and Percentages
1) a) $\frac{4}{5}$ b) $\frac{1}{25}$ c) $\frac{23}{100}$ d) $\frac{999}{1000}$
2) a) $\frac{3}{9}$ b) 0.7
3) $\frac{1}{5}$, 0.5, 55%

Page 19 — Fractions
1) a) $\frac{5}{7}$ b) $\frac{1}{4}$
2) $\frac{2}{3}$ 3) $6\frac{1}{7}$

Page 20 — Fractions
1) $\frac{7}{10}$ 2) a) $\frac{2}{9}$ b) $\frac{6}{12}$ or $\frac{1}{2}$
3) $\frac{63}{6}$ or $\frac{21}{2}$
4) a) $\frac{161}{15}$ or $10\frac{11}{15}$
   b) $\frac{118}{104}$ or $\frac{59}{52}$ or $1\frac{7}{52}$

Page 21 — Fractions
1) 12 m   2) 295   3) $\frac{7}{8}$

Page 22 — Percentage Basics
1) a) 196.95   b) 623
2) a) 75%   b) 160%

Page 23 — Rounding Numbers and Estimating
1) a) 23.6   b) 6.79
2) a) 135.0   b) 4.90

Page 24 — Rounding Numbers and Estimating
1) a) 18   b) 0.26
2) 400   3) 600

Page 25 — Powers and Roots
1) Squares: 4, 9, 16, 25, 36, 49, 64, 81
   Cubes: 8, 27, 64
2) a) 82   b) 11   c) 8

Page 26 — Standard Form
1) a) 1.9×10^7 b) 7.96×10^{-5}

Page 27 — Summary Questions
1) a) 9   b) 8   c) 2
2) a) 15   b) 6
3) −11.8, −0.51, −0.09, 0.001, 0.02, 0.9, 23.91, 54
4) Day 2
5) a) 611   b) 596   c) 2.673
6) a) 122.3   b) 15 120
   c) 0.675   d) 0.0062
7) a) 2489   b) 48
   c) 310.08   d) 5.05
8) a) −2   b) −14
   c) 56   d) −9
9) a) 41, 43, 47   b) 83, 89
10) a) 13, 26, 39, 52, 65
   b) 1, 2, 3, 4, 6, 9, 12, 18, 36
11) $2 \times 2 \times 3 \times 3 \times 7$ or $2^2 \times 3^2 \times 7$
12) 4
13) a) $\frac{6}{10}$ or $\frac{3}{5}$ and 60%
   b) $\frac{65}{100}$ or $\frac{13}{20}$ and 0.65
14) a) E.g. $\frac{6}{10}$ and $\frac{9}{15}$
   b) 60% of 880
15) a) $\frac{5}{8}$ b) $\frac{2}{5}$ c) $\frac{5}{9}$
16) a) $\frac{8}{9}$ b) $\frac{1}{5}$
   c) $\frac{7}{12}$ d) $\frac{20}{33}$
17) a) $1\frac{7}{9}$ (or $\frac{16}{9}$)   b) $1\frac{5}{8}$ (or $\frac{13}{8}$)
   c) $10\frac{1}{8}$ (or $\frac{81}{8}$)   d) −22
18) a) 120   b) 210
   c) 11.7   d) £171
19) a) $\frac{1}{26}$ b) 4%
20) a) 164.4   b) 765 440
21) a) 10   b) 1000
22) a) 76 000   b) 1000
23) 16, 49, 121
24) a) 15.8   b) 14
25) a) 200 000 000
   b) 4.4×10^{-4}
26) 1.7×10^{-5}

Section 2 — Algebra

Page 28 — Algebra — Simplifying Terms
1) a) $3a$ b) $8d$ c) $6x + 2y$
2) a) $-12f$ b) $25x$ c) $3a + b$

Page 29 — Algebra — Simplifying Terms
1) a) d^5 b) $16ef$
   c) p^{10} d) $4j$
2) a) 4 b) 10
   c) $3c^2$ d) $4e^2f^4$

Page 30 — Algebra — Multiplying Out Brackets
1) a) $8 - 2x$ b) $12x - 18y$
2) $1 - 2x$
3) a) $8h - dh$ b) $6j - 2j^2$
   c) $3b^2a - 6b^3$

Page 31 — Algebra — Taking Out Common Factors
1) a) $2(2 - 5r)$ b) $2(3x + y)$
2) a) $6(5s + 2)$
   b) $-8(5 + 3t)$ or $8(-5 - 3t)$
   c) $-4(m + 2n)$
3) a) $a(a + 4)$ b) $3b(3b - 1)$
   c) $3cd(3c + 4d^2)$

Page 32 — Solving Equations
1) a) $x = 3$ b) $x = 11$
   c) $x = 3$ d) $x = 21$
2) a) $x = \frac{3}{4}$ b) $x = \frac{5}{3}$ or $1\frac{2}{3}$
3) a) $x = 20$ b) $x = 1$

Page 33 — Solving Equations
1) $x = -10$ 2) $x = 3$ 3) $x = \frac{8}{3}$

Page 34 — Solving Equations
1) a) $x = 3$ and $x = -3$
   b) $x = 5$ and $x = -5$
   c) $x = 1$ and $x = -1$
2) $x = 0.8$ (to 1 d.p.)

Page 35 — Using Expressions and Formulas
1) $C = 46$ 2) $z = -10$

Page 36 — Making Formulas from Words
1) 3 hours

Page 37 — Number Patterns and Sequences
1) 14 — Subtract 6 from the previous term.

Page 38 — Number Patterns and Sequences
1) a) Multiply the term number by 8 and add 7.
   b) 231
2) $8n + 7$

Page 39 — Inequalities
1) 1, 2, 3, 4
2) a) $x > 2$ b) $x \geq 7$

Page 40 — Inequalities
1) a) 2, 3, 4, 5, 6, 7, 8
   b)

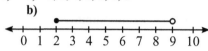

Page 41 — Simultaneous Equations
1) $x = 6, y = 2$
2) a) $3x + 2y = 26, 4x + y = 23$
   b) $x = 4, y = 7$

Page 42 — Summary Questions
1) a) $4a$ b) $9b$ c) $6d + e$
2) a) g^3 b) a^2b^2
   c) $8m^3n^3$ d) $\frac{g}{4}$
3) a) $3v + 24$ b) $-14w - 35$
4) $12y - 18$
5) a) $3(x + 3)$ b) $7(x + 3y)$
6) a) $g(5g - 2)$ b) $6h(1 + 2h)$
   c) $3jk(3j + 5k)$
7) a) $x = 7$ b) $x = 7$
   c) $x = 3$ d) $x = 6$
8) a) $x = \frac{14}{5}$ or $2\frac{4}{5}$ b) $x = 4$
9) a) $x = 2$
   b) $x = 6$ and $x = -6$
   c) $x = 8$ and $x = -8$
10) $x = 6$
11) $y = 8.1$ (to 1 d.p.)
12) 13
13) $q = 9$
14) $P = 7s + 4f$
15) a) 26 — Add 6 to the previous term.
    b) 243 — Multiply the previous term by 3.
    c) 21 — Add the two previous terms together.
16) Multiply the term number by 6 and subtract 3.
17) $2n + 3$
18) 325
19) a) 1, 2, 3, 4, 5, 6
    b) 8, 9, 10, 11
20) $-3, -2, -1, 0, 1, 2, 3, 4, 5$
21) 10
22) a) $-7 > x$ b) $2 < x$
23)

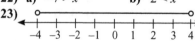

24) $x = 2, y = 5$

Section 3 — Graphs

Page 43 — X and Y Coordinates
1)

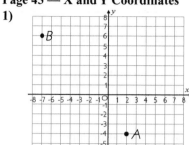

2) $(-1, 0.5)$

Page 44 — Straight Line Graphs
1) a) $x = 2$ b) $y = 4$
2) A line through the origin that slopes steeply downhill.

Page 45 — Plotting Straight Line Graphs
1) a) E.g.

x	0	1	2
y	4	2	0

   b)

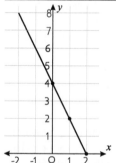

Page 46 — Plotting Straight Line Graphs
1) a) When $x = 0$, $y = 2$ and when $y = 0$, $x = -1$
   b)

Page 47 — Reading Off Graphs
1) $y = 2.4$

Page 48 — Conversion Graphs
1) 2 inches

Page 49 — Solving Simultaneous Equations
1) a)
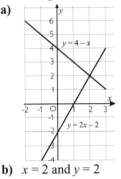
b) $x = 2$ and $y = 2$

Page 50 — Quadratic Graphs
1) a)
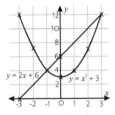
b) $(-1, 4)$ and $(3, 12)$

Page 51 — Summary Questions
1) $A(2, 2)$ $B(3, -2)$
$C(-2, -3)$ $D(-2, 1)$
2) $(-2, -1)$
3) $(2.5, 0)$
4) a) E.g. $(4, 1)$ b) E.g. $(1, 2)$
5) $(3, 1)$
6) E.g. $x = 3$ and $x = 5$
7) a) Neither
   b) Downhill
   c) Uphill
8)
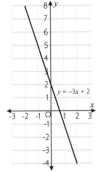
9) When $x = 0$, $y = 10$ and when $y = 0$, $x = 5$
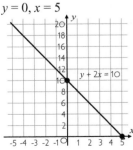

10) Draw a straight line from one axis to the graph, then draw a straight line down or across to the other axis.
11) a) On his way home.
   b) 15 minutes
12) a) 300 euros   b) 500 pounds
13)
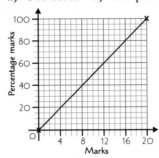

14)
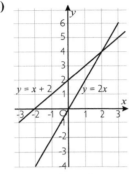
$x = 2$ and $y = 4$
15) Parabola
16) a)

x	-3	-2	-1	0	1	2	3
y	6	1	-2	-3	-2	1	6

b), c)
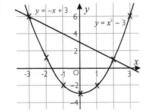

d) $x = 2$ and $y = 1$
$x = -3$ and $y = 6$

Section 4 —
Ratio, Proportion and Rates of Change

Page 52 — Ratios
1) a) $1:9$ b) $2:5$ c) $5:3$

Page 53 — Ratios
1) 35 litres
2) 126
3) $4:3$

Page 54 — Ratios
1) £240

Page 55 — Direct Proportion
1) 39   2) 9 kg
3) 378 g oats, 180 g butter, 150 g sugar

Page 56 — Percentage Change
1) a) $15 000   b) 150%
2) 6.25%

Page 57 — Percentage Change
1) 3150 m
2) 18 °C

Page 58 — Metric and Imperial Units
1) a) 35 mm   b) 2800 cm^3
   c) 4500 kg
2) a) 20 kg   b) 150 cm
   c) 12.5 miles

Page 59 — Converting Units
1) 4.2 cm, 44 mm, 0.5 m
2) a) 41.6 km   b) 41 600 m
   c) 4 160 000 cm

Page 60 — More Conversions
1) a) 2400 mm^3 b) 40 m^2
2) 96 km/h

Page 61 — Reading Scales and Estimating
1) 12.5 ml
2) a) cm   b) kg   c) km

Page 62 — Time
1) 3 months 13 days

Page 63 — Maps and Scale Drawings
1) 1 cm by 2 cm

Page 64 — Bearings
1) 102°   2) 282°

Page 65 — Speed
1) 12 km/h   2) 15 km/h

Page 66 — Summary Questions
1) a) $7:8$ b) $3:2$ c) $8:7$
2) $1:3.6$
3) 50
4) £105
5) £1.25
6) £70
7) 16%
8) See page 58
9) a) 50 miles   b) 75 cm
10) 10 000 g
11) a) 0.2 m   b) 60 cm^2
12) 180 000 mm^3
13) 43.2 km/h
14) 27.5 kg
15) E.g. grams (g)
16) 1 litre

17) 280 minutes
18) 4 cm
19) 50 m by 25 m
20)

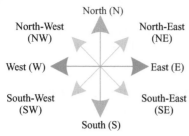

21) 064°
22) 244°
23) 75 km
24) 4 km/h
25) 6.25 km/h

Section 5 — Geometry and Measures

Page 67 — Symmetry
1) 1   **2)** 2

Page 68 — Quadrilaterals
1) Kite

Page 69 — Triangles and Regular Polygons
1) 20 lines of symmetry, order of rotational symmetry = 20

Page 70 — Perimeter and Area
1) 4 m and 3 m   **2)** 40 cm²

Page 71 — Area of Compound Shapes
1) 45 cm²

Page 72 — Circles
1) Circumference = 62.8 mm (1 d.p.)
Area = 314.2 mm² (1 d.p.)
2) 8.74 cm (3 s.f.)

Page 73 — Circle Problems
1)

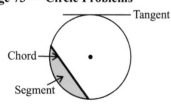

2) 137.44 cm² (2 d.p.)
3) 15.5 cm² (1 d.p.)

Page 74 — 3D Shapes
1) **a)** Regular tetrahedron
b) Faces = 4, edges = 6

Page 75 — Nets and Surface Area
1) 96 cm²

Page 76 — Nets and Surface Area
1) E.g.

2) 12 cm²

Page 77 — Volume
1) 168 cm³

Page 78 — Angle Basics
1) **a)** obtuse **b)** reflex **c)** acute

Page 79 — Geometry Rules
1) $x = 25°$

Page 80 — Intersecting and Parallel Lines
1) $y = 102°$

Page 81 — Geometry Problems
1) $BEF = 100°$

Page 82 — Exterior and Interior Angles
1) Exterior angle = 45°
Interior angle = 135°

Page 83 — Transformations
1) A translation of 2 units right and 7 units down.

Page 84 — Transformations
1) **a)** and **b)**

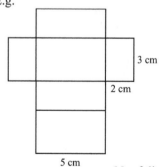

2) Rotation of 90° (a quarter turn) anticlockwise about point (–2, –1).

Page 85 — Transformations
1) 3

Page 86 — Constructions
1) E.g.

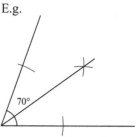

Page 87 — Triangle Construction
1)

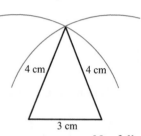

Not full size

Page 88 — Pythagoras' Theorem
1) 13 cm

Page 89 — Summary Questions
1) Lines of symmetry = 2
Order of rotational symmetry = 2
2) E.g. rhombus and parallelogram
3) Octagon
4) Perimeter = 32 cm, area = 55 cm²
5) 120 cm²
6) 30 cm²
7) 201.06 cm² (2 d.p.)
8) 22.6 cm² (1 d.p.)
9) Faces = 6, edges = 12
10) E.g.

Not full size
Volume = 30 cm³
Surface area = 62 cm²
11) 48 cm³
12) **a)** E.g. 72°
(any value above 0° and below 90°)
b) E.g. 111°
(any value above 90° and below 180°)
c) E.g. 260°
(any value above 180° and below 360°)

3) Alternate angles

4) $x = 40°$

5) Exterior angle = 36°
Interior angle = 144°

6) 1080°

7) 4, 3

8) (3, 0)

9) (5, 3), (14, 3) and (11, 12)

10)

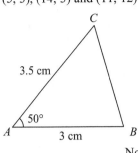

Not full size

11) 7.14 cm (3 s.f.)

12) 5 (units)

Section 6 — Probability and Statistics

Page 90 — Probability

1) **a)** 0.1 or $\frac{1}{10}$ **b)** 0.5 or $\frac{1}{2}$

  c) 0.5 or $\frac{1}{2}$

Page 91 — Probability

1) $\frac{15}{36} = \frac{5}{12}$
(In your table, put the results of adding the scores in the cells.)

2) 12

Page 92 — Experimental Probability

1) Red = 0.43, blue = 0.24, green = 0.33

Page 93 — Data and Tables

1) $\frac{2}{16} = \frac{1}{8}$

Page 94 — Sorting Information

1)

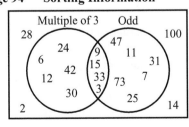

Page 95 — Sorting Information

1)

	Multiple of 5	Not a multiple of 5
Factor of 20	5, 10	1, 2, 4
Not a factor of 20	15	0, 3, 6, 7, 8, 9, 11, 12, 13, 14

Page 96 — Graphs and Charts

1) 16

Page 97 — Graphs and Charts

1)

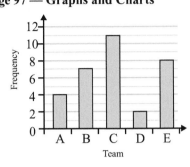

Page 98 — Mean, Median, Mode and Range

1) Median = 11, Mode = 12,
Mean = 11, Range = 7

Page 99 — Averages from Frequency Tables

1) Mode = 1, Range = 3, Mean = 1.25,
Median = 30.5th value = 1

Page 100 — Averages from Frequency Diagrams

1) Mode = 4, Range = 4,
Mean = 2.93 (to 2 d.p.), Median = 3

Page 101 — Scatter Graphs

1) About 4 years

Page 102 — Summary Questions

1) A probability of 1 means that something is certain to happen.

2) $\frac{5}{12}$

3) P(lose) = 0.9

4)

	Second spin	
First spin	Black	White
Black	BB	BW
White	WB	WW

5) 10

---

6) Experimental Probability = $\dfrac{\text{Frequency}}{\text{Number of times you tried}}$

7) Data that can only take countable values.

8) 9 people

9)

	3 sides	Not 3 sides
All straight sides	C, E	A, F
Not all straight sides	D	B

10)

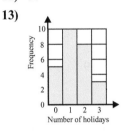

11) The number of things in each category.

12) 10

13)

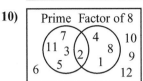

14) Mode = 5, Median = 5,
Mean = 6, Range = 9

15) Mode = 2, Median = 2,
Mean = 2, Range = 4

16) Mode = 4
Total lengths swum = 76
Total children = 24
Mean = 3.17 (to 2 d.p.)

17) (Strong) negative correlation

18) 35

Index